THE WAR ON WORDS

TEN WORDS EVERY CHRISTIAN SHOULD FIGHT FOR

DAVID DE BRUYN

The War on Words: Ten Words Every Christian Should Fight For
Copyright © 2023 by David de Bruyn

Published by G3 Press
4979 GA-5
Douglasville, GA 30135
www.G3Min.org

All rights reserved. No part of this publication may be reproduced, stored in a retrieval system, or transmitted in any form by any means, electronic, mechanical, photocopy, recording, or otherwise, without prior permission of the publisher, except as provided for by USA copyright law.

Scripture quotations are from the ESV® Bible (*The Holy Bible, English Standard Version*®), copyright © 2001 by Crossway, a publishing ministry of Good News Publishers. Used by permission. All rights reserved. All emphases in Scripture quotations have been added by the author.

Printed in the United States of America by Graphic Response, Atlanta, GA.

ISBN: 978-1-959908-10-4

Cover Design: Scott Schaller

CONTENTS

Acknowledgements i

Introduction iii

1 Authentic 1

2 Authority 31

3 Culture 61

4 Emotion 91

5 Equality 125

6 Freedom 145

7 Hate 167

8 Relevance 191

9 Taste 211

10 Tolerance 243

    Conclusion 253

ACKNOWLEDGEMENTS

These chapters originally appeared as weekly blog posts on the website of Religious Affections Ministries. I'm thankful for Dr. Scott Aniol's invitation to write and post there for several years.

Mark Swedberg offered to edit a draft version of this book and did so with precision and excellence. My grateful thanks to him for his labor.

INTRODUCTION

Words are not just names. If they were, we'd never argue about them. We'd simply swap out one label for another. The problem is that words are things with meaning. Yes, they are man-made things, concatenations of syllables created by human cultures, and the particular meaning has been shaped through convention and association. But words are things that carry meaning, and correct meaning is at the heart of worship and obedience.

When the thing in question distorts meaning, it becomes a very dangerous thing. A road-sign that points left when it should point right is a dangerous thing. A box of rat-poison labelled "jellybeans" is a dangerous thing. When words are used badly or wrongly, it is not simply a matter of some grammar that needs polishing. Mangled words are more like a loose nut in an airplane engine, like a stray flu-germ on the chef's hands. As Mark Twain put it, "The difference between the *almost right* word and the *right* word is really a large matter: 'tis the difference between the lightning bug and the lightning."

Words are the stock and trade of pastors. They should care more than the average man about word meanings, both denotative and connotative. They should oppose the wrong use of words as the apostles did when false teachers distorted the words "liberty" (2 Peter 2:19), "grace" (Jude 1:4) and "people of God" (Philippians 3:1-3).

To be careless about words is to fail to see their importance. It is, to invoke the old medieval debate, choosing nominalism over realism. Nominalism tends to deny ultimate realities or fixed meanings, and sees names as just convenient labels we use to impose meanings. Realism believes God's reality is in and of itself meaningful and that meaning is more or less discoverable. In God's case, however, naming precedes creating: God spoke, naming the creation, and it came to be. Meaning or naming preceded the existence of the thing; the name was not a mere interpretation after the fact. He then gave man the privilege of assigning further names to creation. There is a true correspondence, such Realism would say, between naming and nature.

The meanings of the words *tolerance, freedom, authority, authentic, relevant, culture, equality, emotion, taste,* and *hate* are not arbitrary and purely subjective. Nor are they unimportant. These words are currently the words at the very center of our culture and at the root of disputes about worship, ministry, missions, social justice, morality, economics, and Christian living. To get the wrong meaning about these words will likely be to court failure or disaster in ministry. Church leaders cannot afford to live with the mangled form of these words.

INTRODUCTION

Is this being "obsessed with disputes and arguments over words" (1 Timothy 6:4)? I trust not. It is the job of those whose primary tool is the written and spoken word to refuse to allow these words to fall into enemy hands. As Luther said, "If I profess with loudest voice and clearest exposition every portion of the truth of God except that little point which the world and the Devil are at that moment attacking, I am not confessing Christ, however boldly I may be professing Christ. Where the battle rages, there the loyalty of the soldier is proved, and to be steady on all the battlefield besides, is mere flight and disgrace if he flinches at that point." May we earnestly contend for the true meaning of these ten words.

Words are more than names. Words are things that either correspond to something in reality or fail to. When words fail to correspond to something true about God's reality, they become part of the darkening of human understanding. Like a sign pointing the wrong way, like a faulty map, the mangled word gives the human mind a false inner reality and distorts the truth.

1

AUTHENTIC

Few words roll off the modern tongue as readily or as frequently as the family of words associated with *authentic*. *Authenticity, real, sincere,* and *intentional* are like newly minted gold for the Millennial tongue. Most previous generations of humans would have looked at you with furrowed eyebrows and pained expressions of confusion, had you greeted them with the line, "Keep it real, bro!"

Only a narcissistic generation would imagine that it had stumbled upon the meaning of authenticity, and that those that went before them were hopelessly mired in inauthentic, fake, insincere ways of life. But Xers, Yers and Millennials can barely contain their glee at how real they're keepin' it.

We buy Fair-Trade coffee, eat organic, listen to indie music, practice yoga, post online testimonials, blog about ourselves and our "struggles," take natural medicines, wear mass-produced jeans distressed to appear "vintage," seek out pristine vacation spots, and one of the highest compliments we can pay someone is to say, "He seems really sincere."

This has bled into the church with its own manifestations: accountability groups, informality in worship, a general suspicion of formality and tradition as insincere, a therapeutic approach to ministry, and seeking very different emotional experiences in corporate worship.

Of course, the culture is not aiming at nothing when it makes authenticity its goal, however blurry its general eyesight might be. In a consumer culture, we are bombarded with advertisements and marketing that is the very opposite of truthfulness. A consumer culture lives on fakery, exaggeration, hype, and artificially created discontent. At some point, a kind of fatigue sets in with all the attempts to charm us out of our pocketbook, and authenticity-hunting becomes a kind of consolation that we haven't been duped by it all.

Similarly, the Bible has much to say about phoniness and hypocrisy. From Moses to Paul, the Bible condemns religion that is a mere facade for an unchanged heart. A hypocrite, in Greek culture, was literally a stage-actor, and the word came to describe those who maintain religious exteriors for the sake of pleasing man, gaining money or power, or something else. Heart-religion is indeed a Scriptural concern, and that is all the more reason to rescue *authentic* from its mangled misrepresentations.

To do so, quite a bit of rust needs to be scraped off these words. First, we'll need to rescue formalism from the accusation that it is insincere, along with its corollary that informality and casualness are the natural state of sincerity. Second, we'll need to distinguish between sincerity and emotion. Third, we'll need to restore the difference between Scriptural honesty and the modern therapeutic model of counseling, and we'll need to critique the idea that one's natural thoughts and feelings are truthful and should be shared.

SINCERELY AMUSED

It's a supreme irony, or perhaps a sad blindness, that the present generation is supposedly in love with "authenticity," "sincerity," and "keeping it real." After all, we've been doing everything *but* that for nearly a century. As Neil Postman pointed out in *Amusing Ourselves to Death*, we took a medium designed for amusing spectacle — theater — and used technology to turn it into the dominant medium of our time. First film, then television, and now the web, have transformed the most serious moments of life into forms of amusement to be watched by a popcorn-eating crowd. Politics has gone from thoughtful debate watched by patient and intelligent crowds, to a cage-fight, with commentators, bookies, and soundbites made for TV and the web. The Courts have become reality-TV sideshows for us to laugh at the sassy judge's replies. Warfare has become a televised sports match, with blow-by-blow commentators and action replays. Counseling has become a bizarre exercise in voyeuristic curiosity, as we hear strangers' problems, and watch the psychologist untangle the messed-up lives of other people. Education has become films of amusing characters, fun computer games, and amusing activities that suit each one's "learning style."

The most serious, or *sincere* part of our TV experience is supposed to be "the News," where men and women in suits and corporate wear speak in sober monotones to "give us the facts." Stories of human suffering, terror and tragedy are literally sold to us as a thirty-minute entertainment product paid for by advertisers and, consequently, filled with stories that scare, enrage, or excite — the kind that garner viewers or listeners. No one notices the weird incongruity when we go from hearing about chemical warfare in Syria to fun commercials advertising cosmetics, diapers, cars, and insurance. (Imagine King Nebuchadnezzar in his throne room receiving word of enemies coming from the west, and every few moments, a court jester running in singing, or showing off something from Babylon's market.) With the recent political shenanigans and the hysterical "news media" that accompanied it, some of the makeup is beginning to drip off that pig. People are beginning to realize that "the News" was always a sideshow masquerading as serious conversation, flattering our view of ourselves as thoughtful people, where, in reality, we were drawn in by the entertainment of alarmism and sold to advertisers. There is nothing really sincere or authentic about all this.

AUTHENTIC

It was inevitable, I suppose, that we should end up with Reality TV. When serious information is just one more show, we start pining for something without actors. Supposedly setting up a camera in a home, or on an island, or in a car, will make the "story" more interesting, more "real." Actually, it's a sign of the law of diminishing returns. Once those shows that only mimic life no longer scratch the itch, we want life itself to be the show. Note, the move to reality television is not people wanting "reality;" this is people wanting *reality-as-entertainment*.

With the ubiquity of screens, cameras, and social media, we're all now in a reality show. So we have reached the place where people film themselves in a place or performing some activity and only really enjoy the moment when it's played back on a screen to them, or placed online. It's as if the screen has become a priest, a mediator. We can no longer get at life through our five senses; we must film ourselves and then live vicariously through the act of watching ourselves again. Spectacle has become our perception of reality, and we even need to be spectators of our own actions. We cannot even enjoy the simple and the mundane on our own; we must publicize it for the entertainment of others on some social media platform, and only when they comment or "like" or smiley-face it, do we feel validated. We have to entertain others or be entertained to even feel that these moments were "real." Entertainment is no longer what people do when not engaged in work, it has become their means of perception, their source of identity, their very experience of reality.

So what should we make of all these cries for "authenticity," "sincerity," and "reality?" On the one hand, they are clearly preposterous. People gorging themselves on junk food are not yet serious when they talk about health, and people immersed in amusement are not yet serious when they talk about *the real world*. On the other hand, there is in them probably a true longing for something other than life-as-amusement, although they are ignorant of what it might be. When people are feeling bored with life, worn out by images, de-sensitized to shock-value, they aren't sure if they need another shot of entertainment, or an emetic.

I've heard it said that Millennials and Gen-Zers are particularly relational because of their social-media savvy. That, in turn, makes them more "authentic" in relationships. If that means they actually spend time with people, put their phones away, stop instagramming and snapchatting every moment, look up from their screens and have meaningful conversations with the other person two meters away from them, then I'd agree. If not, then they are the natural descendants and logical consequence of a twentieth-century generation that made amusement its goal in life. The difference is that now its kids get to carry that once-bulky TV in their pocket and watch it at every available moment. When I was a kid, we at least had the social experience of fighting over the remote. If self-absorption behind a TV has been succeeded by self-absorption while lost in social media, not much has improved. In fact, the illusion of relationships taking place through these screens has only made the alienation from others more severe.

In truth, behind the lust for the amusement of spectacle is a profound selfishness, even a narcissism. When seeking amusement, I do not seek to give, to share, to bless, or to grow. I seek only the merest titillation of myself. When this is the dominant form of cultural life, you are dealing with the most loveless generation to see the sun.

We can never become serious about "being authentic" until we are willing to abandon entertainment as our mode of worship, communication, or education. Until we see that the spectacles we use to view the world have become screens, we will not notice their ubiquity. (I once went into a sports-themed restaurant and counted around twenty screens from where I was sitting—I was told there were more. And the patrons still had their own screens on their tables in their phones and tablets. At what point do we call this a kind of madness, or sickness?)

If we really desire to "do life," to "be authentic," to "keep it real," it begins by repenting of our slavery to the god of entertainment, confessing that we have looked to it for life. We should repent that we have wished that worship, marriage, parenting, work, and obedience could be mediated to us through the mode of passive amusement. To put it another way, we should repent that we have kept ourselves at the center of our lives and loved our own amusement more than God or neighbor. The confession of evil works is the beginning of good works, and being *real* begins with turning away from the narcissistic insincerity of entertainment as the mainstay of our lives.

WHAT TITUS FOUND IN THE MOST HOLY

When Titus attacked Jerusalem in A.D. 66–70, before ordering its destruction, Titus entered the Most Holy Place to see for himself what was really hidden behind that veil. He found, to his dismay, nothing besides the Mercy Seat. There was "nothing there."

Titus is like many modern Christians—intoxicated with the idea of "sincerity," "authenticity," and "realness." These Christians similarly wish to strip away what they call "masks," remove what they consider inauthentic, or even phony, so that we can get at the *real reality*. You'll hear them speak about the "curse of religiosity," about people "hiding behind traditions."

What are these masks, in their opinion? Usually, it is any kind of (older) custom, ritual, tradition, or form. If something doesn't seem to be transparent to the mind, colloquial in expression, informal or casual in approach, it seems opaque to their impatient desire for immediate comprehension. They reason that if something is slowing you down when it comes to perception, it must be a deliberate attempt to obscure, befuddle, or even lord it over you. The "keep-it-real" man is almost always a populist, suspicious of what is not easily perceivable. And if there is an easier, more casual, more informal way of saying the same thing, he concludes that every instance of formalism is some kind of posturing, some desire to be aloof and make it more difficult than it has to be.

It could be a dress code for the pulpit. It could be singing songs with exalted language. It could be preaching in a dignified manner, or even from behind an elevated pulpit. It could be architecture that represents classical Christian ideas. It could be following a set order of service. It could be hymns with dense lyrics, or unfamiliar melodies. It could be a more formal prayer to God.

For the authenticity hound, this is all smoke and mirrors. For him, formal language, formal orders of service, formal approaches to God, chivalry, manners and customs are moves towards unreality. He suspects that the Christians and the leaders doing these things refuse to "be themselves." After all, he has spoken to them outside of Sunday services, and they are "normal" then. So, what can all this be except an act of some kind? How could the same man adopt two different modes of speech for different occasions? Isn't that the mark of an actor?

The reason the authenticity hound concludes these things is that he has been enculturated by the counterculture. He believes that the more immediate and unrehearsed the self-expression, the more honest it must be. Rehearsed, planned, or formal expression involves forethought and is, therefore, guilty-on-sight of calculated posturing. To him, spontaneous expression prevents insincerity from intruding because it just expels out the mouth whatever is on the mind—there is no time to rehearse. This is supposedly the mark of honest people—those willing to be "vulnerable," "transparent," "out there."

Of course, this would make the poetry of David an exercise in faked piety because poetry is almost never spontaneous. It would make the Lord's Prayer an exercise in masks because it is known and rehearsed. It would make the Bible itself less-than-authentic, for every book was carefully written following a literary form.

What the sincerity-junkie cannot see is that there are reasons for formality other than posturing, hypocrisy, or evasion. A suit and tie at a funeral, a wedding-dress and vows at a wedding, opening a door for a lady, using titles for people in authority, table manners, an eloquent love-letter, or a poem are not exercises in deception. They are the ways we "dress-up" physical reality to signify greater realities. A form may not be *hiding* reality, it may in fact be *clothing* it with beauty and significance. That is, formality is often a way of improving something ordinary, adorning it with beauty, so that we now see something more than just the physical thing. We see what it represents, what it envisions. We see man made in God's image, not merely the physical man of the dust.

Though his writing is dense, I heartily recommend reading this extended quote by Richard Weaver. Writing in the 1940s, Weaver perfectly defines and explains the motives of the Realness Police:

> That culture is sentiment refined and measured by intellect becomes clear as we turn our attention to a kind of barbarism appearing in our midst and carrying unmistakable power to disintegrate. This threat is best described as the desire of immediacy, for its aim is to dissolve the formal aspects of everything and to get at the supposititious reality behind them. It is characteristic of the barbarian, whether he appears in a precultural stage or emerges from below into the waning day of a civilization, to insist upon seeing a thing "as it is." The desire testifies that he has nothing in himself with which to spiritualize it; the relation is one of thing to thing without the intercession of imagination. Impatient of the veiling with which the man of higher type gives the world imaginative meaning, the barbarian and the Philistine, who is the barbarian

living amid culture, demands the access of immediacy. Where the former wishes representation, the latter insists upon starkness of materiality, suspecting rightly that forms will mean restraint. . . .

The member of a culture, on the other hand, purposely avoids the relationship of immediacy; he wants the object somehow depicted and fictionized, or, as Schopenhauer expressed it, he wants not the thing but the idea of the thing. He is embarrassed when this is taken out of its context of proper sentiments and presented bare, for he feels that this is a reintrusion of that world which his whole conscious effort has sought to banish. Forms and conventions are the ladder of ascent. And hence the speechlessness of the man of culture when he beholds the barbarian tearing aside some veil which is half adornment, half concealment. He understands what is being done, but he cannot convey the understanding because he cannot convey the idea of sacrilege. His cries of *abeste profani* are not heard by those who in the exhilaration of breaking some restraint feel that they are extending the boundaries of power or of knowledge.

Every group regarding itself as emancipated is convinced that its predecessors were fearful of reality. It looks upon euphemisms and all the veils of decency with which things were previously draped as obstructions which it, with superior wisdom and praiseworthy courage, will now strip away. Imagination and indirection, it identifies with obscurantism; the mediate is an enemy to freedom.... Barbarism and Philistinism cannot see that knowledge of material reality is a knowledge of death. The desire to get ever closer to the source of physical sensation—this is the downward pull which puts an end to ideational life.[1]

THE COLLOQUIAL, THE CASUAL, AND THE CRAFTED

Those who call for "authenticity," "realness," and "sincerity," are not always sure what they mean if you press them for a definition. Some mean honesty, others mean integrity, both of which are virtues the Bible commends and commands. But some of those calling for authenticity are really calling for a removal of formality from worship, communication, and life in general. Things formal are considered posed and vain and, therefore, less than real. (Of course, objecting to what is supposedly posed and vain is a tad rich when coming from the take-a-selfie-and-edit-the-photo generation, but let's leave that aside, for the moment.) People like this believe that any move towards informality is a move towards honesty and openness.

---

[1] Richard M. Weaver, *Ideas Have Consequences* (Chicago, IL: University of Chicago Press, 1948), 23, 25–26.

Casualness in dress, colloquialism in speech, and the absence of structure means everyone is being more spontaneous and "authentic." Notice how many church websites advertise their meetings by promising a "relaxed atmosphere," as if other churches are deliberately seeking a *tense* atmosphere. What these churches are really doing is agreeing that whatever feels formal (and, therefore, unspontaneous, and perhaps unfamiliar) has no place in "authentic" worship, and that the more familiar and casual it seems, the more it is "connecting," and "real."

A few years ago, a book came out that, in my opinion, made some remarkable observations. *Doing Our Own Thing* (with the subtitle, *The Degradation of Music and Language and Why We Should, Like, Care*) is written by John McWhorter, who, to my knowledge, makes no claim to be a Christian. McWhorter uses examples of letters, speeches, and debates to point to a major shift in our culture. He shows that, until recently, most cultures have spoken in two voices. One voice is the everyday, conversational street language, with its slang, colloquialisms, repetition, and impreciseness. Everyday conversation includes a lot of hedging ("like," "sort of," "kind of like," "y'know"), grammatical mistakes, and colloquial expressions. McWhorter has no complaint about this (nor do I), and documents historical examples of how the language on the street or in the kitchen has always been one voice that the culture uses.

AUTHENTIC

The other voice is the voice used for speeches, written prose, sermons, and even letters. This form is eloquent, refined, precise, and polished. Its tone is produced by carefully crafted words, adopted for specific occasions. It is quite remarkable to read the letters written by Civil War soldiers to their loved ones at home. The same men who would be speaking in a coarse and ragged manner on the battlefield, would write home in tones of surprising eloquence and literary polish. Clearly, nineteenth-century men did not think that it was hypocrisy to use two different tones for different purposes and different audiences.

McWhorter shows, using examples of speeches and letters, that the tone of formal oratory and prose has been tending towards the conversational and colloquial since the 1960s. Speeches by senators in the 40s and in the early 2000s are markedly different. The formal tone is disappearing almost completely from our society. McWhorter suggests that the counter-culture revolution of the 1960s enshrined informality and turned the wider culture against any form of artifice. Language that is carefully written, artfully constructed, and poetic in quality has come to be viewed as inauthentic, staged, and one more attempt by some intellectuals to lord it over the common man. Sincerity, authenticity, and keeping it real, is represented by an off-the-cuff, everyday style in speaking and writing. Once again, McWhorter is not raging against the conversational language we all use. He is asking why those domains where language used to put on its Sunday best now prefer that it be in beach-clothes.

This has major implications for Christians and for Christian leaders. When we consider the prayers of the psalms, are these colloquial, conversational prayers, or are they eloquently written? Undoubtedly, David spoke to his soldiers in everyday language, but when he addressed God in poetry, and, particularly, when he represented the nation in prayer, he adopted an elevated tone. Or consider the following: are the sermons of Scripture, such as the book of Hebrews, informal "chats," or are they carefully written examples of rhetoric? Remove the tone of eloquent address from a culture, and you have hamstrung it from being able to have reverent worship.

To turn again to Richard Weaver, we find a gem of insight in this statement: "Unformed expression is ever tending toward ignorance." To put it another way, when people wish to express themselves in the tone of carefulness and reverence (as worship certainly requires), their expression needs the guidance of *form*. Speeches need introductions, propositional statements, main points, illustrations, supporting arguments, conclusions, and an elevated vocabulary. Poetry needs a particular meter, rhyme scheme, line length, metaphor, and other devices. Whatever the device used for human expression, it has a form that such expression must be poured into, like water into a mold. Apart from the mold, water will simply splatter randomly on the floor.

Weaver is suggesting that human expression is just like that. Remove the artifices of form (which the formal tone of address requires), and human expression tends towards ignorance, which is exactly why the casual and colloquial tone is not where we find the clearest thought or the deepest insight. If the thoughts and sentiments of people are never channelled by the discipline of formal speech or poetry, they tend to become disorganized, disparate, and, in a word, chaotic. And chaos does not enlighten or educate anyone, nor is it more real, authentic, or sincere. Think of the following examples: the unprepared extemporaneous preacher, the painful testimony time monopolized by one long-winded and imprecise person, the rambling and circuitous public prayer, and "what this verse means to me" Bible studies. Ironically, when churches tolerate or foster this kind of thing in the name of sincerity and authenticity, the fog of ignorance and vacuousness of thought that grows is doing the very opposite of *getting to the heart of things*, or increasing "transparency," "realness," and authenticity.

In my own life, I have experienced the difference it has made to recognize and practice these two tones. During the day, I cannot pray as succinctly or concisely as I might like, so my prayer is made up of momentary phrases, short observations, even unarticulated sentiments—a lot more conversational and colloquial, without, I hope, being irreverent. But in times of private devotion, I have found that a short, carefully worded, "prayer of address" is far more helpful to thoughtful worship than a lot of rambling conversational prayer and consequent wandering of mind. Like a letter, such a prayer cannot be long, for most of us cannot sustain that kind of precision for very long. But the clarity, reverence, and, ironically, *sincerity* it brings has been very helpful to me. This also explains why Christians have often written down some of their prayers, because they are artfully-composed addresses to God. No one writes down his conversational impromptu prayers, nor have the sermons of ramblers been recorded for posterity.

Similarly in corporate worship, well-written hymns, well-thought-out prayers, well-crafted sermons, and other well-prepared aspects of corporate worship are not acts of hypocrisy, posturing, or quenching the Spirit. They respect form, and use it for beauty, reverence, and precise expression. Where form is respected and steadily explained, it not only shapes our expression, it further refines it. Long-term exposure to well-formed expression has a maturing effect on our own. Our minds start to think in those forms. We find ourselves praying better prayers. Our spontaneous testimonies are more succinct, and more edifying. Our extemporaneous teaching has substance. But when we adopt only the colloquial tone for our corporate worship, we will end up losing not only the thoughtfulness and beauty of the elevated tone, but coherence and substance in the conversational tone also.

SINCERITY AND PROFANITY

Many pastors and Christian leaders believe they are purifying Christianity and worship when they remove any kind of formality from corporate worship. Formal dress, an exalted tone in prayer, or reverent music are eschewed for a more casual and informal approach. They appear to believe that retaining forms that are not immediately recognizable or penetrable by the average Christian represents an attempt to "appear religious." To them, this is hollow priestcraft and chicanery. In fact, the term *hocus pocus* grew out of the medieval peasant's presence at the Mass where he would hear the priest say, "This is the body of Christ." In Latin this is, *"hoc est corpus Christi."* At some point, the *hoc est corpus* got mangled into *hocus pocus*. How bread became God was a kind of magic, impenetrable to the average peasant. Many modern Christian leaders believe divesting Christianity of formality will purify it of hocus pocus and make it more sincere, authentic, and real. But this profoundly misunderstands the difference between the profane and the sacred.

Since Cain and Abel, man has understood that when something is performed, offered, or used in an act of worship, that thing is set apart for that purpose. It is sacred. It is not always intrinsically so; it becomes sacred because it is so dedicated. It is sacred in purpose, not in makeup. This applies to animals, altars, human bodies, clothing, spaces, music, speech, times, even whole days or weeks or entire buildings. This is the act of consecration: setting things apart for holy uses. Once a common thing or place or time is set apart for worship, it is considered sacred.

The Mosaic Law made this point in hundreds of ways. Ordinary animals, utensils, tents, and clothes would be consecrated and re-consecrated through sacrifices and ritual cleansings. When something was not consecrated or ritually cleansed, it was not to be used in worship, with dire penalties for disobedience. God kept explaining that by these acts of separating the ordinary from the sacred, Israel would be taught that God is holy: "That you may distinguish between holy and unholy, and between unclean and clean" (Leviticus 10:10). God is other. And because He is other, He is not known or worshipped by what is purely familiar or common. Even in pagan worship, common things, such as shoes were to be left in front of the temple (Latin= *pro fanum*), not brought inside it. To bring the unconsecrated into a sacred space was to profane that space, and indeed, that god. To obliterate this distinction between what was specifically given for worship, and what was for use in ordinary life was an act of profaning the name of the Lord. To profane God is to drag God and His worship down to the level of the ordinary.

No one, in all these millennia, misunderstood the nature of sacred things. They knew that the wood of the altar is still wood. They knew that anointing oil is still oil, and that the Sabbath is another twenty-four hours like all others. They did not waste time pointing out that priestly linen was the same material as regular linen. Nevertheless, they knew that what was consecrated had changed in its purpose, and since that purpose was now sacred, the objects or space or time were to be considered such.

Although the New Testament church is no longer restricted to a Tabernacle or Temple, and although it is true that all of our lives are to be offered up as worship, this does not mean that we by this fact lose the distinction between the sacred and the profane—particularly regarding corporate worship. Romans 12:1 is not meant to profane worship; it is meant to consecrate the mundane. The Lord's Day is still His day. Ministers still ought to dress as if they were handling the most serious message in the world. Christians still ought to dress as if they were going to appear before God. Prayer still ought to be speech set apart to speak to the Most High. The Bible still ought to be read and heard like no other book. The space we meet in still ought to be treated like a space given over to worship. In various ways, we New Testament believers still ought to show that what we set apart for worship has a consecrated purpose, and, therefore, we should treat it as sacred, not as common.

The realness police do not understand this. They rightly recognize that all of life is sacred, but then they take this to mean that the difference between worship and life is precisely what they should eliminate. They must make worship seem as "real" or familiar as driving, eating, or walking through the mall. That way, they reason, no pretence exists in worship.

But in fact, such people turn out to be destroyers. Their efforts do not elevate normal life to a state of consecration; instead, they debase everything. Instead of a deep sense of reality permeating worship, they end up with a profound sense of mundaneness in corporate worship. Instead of filling the Christian church with sincerity, they fill it with what is average. Life does not become elevated and consecrated; worship becomes predictable, every day, and ordinary. Awe and reverence are lost, and the small consolation is that "we're all so real about it." Like Titus, they tear away the veil, find nothing is there, and feel satisfied that at least they removed the mask.

The very contrast between worship and everyday life is exactly what invests worship with its power and transformative force. The gap between the common and the sacred is what makes worship a numinous and spiritual experience. The sacredness of worship is precisely what engenders the fear of the Lord. When we tear away at form—

those things and ways and acts that remind us that this occasion is sacred—we tear away at worship itself. Indeed, we tear away at our own dignity as being made in the image of God, not merely animals concerned with the material. When we refuse the distinction between the sacred and the common, we are nothing more than what C. S. Lewis called *trousered apes*.

Do not despise consecration. Do not attribute the setting apart of worship as a sacred experience as a bunch of sham and pretence. Learn to embrace such consecration yourself. Recognize it is part of the way God teaches us that He Himself is holy.

AS REAL AS I FEEL

An assumption of a generation intoxicated with authenticity is the notion that feelings don't lie. Given their spontaneous and often uncontrollable nature, emotions are seen as the inevitable and unstoppable eruptions of the heart. Breaking through the surface layer of "masks," "forms," or some other supposed act of evading one's inner truth, emotions represent pure, authentic, sincerity. You'll find this all over modern culture and, sadly, modern Christianity.

Witness the pop songs about "admitting how we feel about each other," "surrender to what our hearts want," "these feelings don't lie." A whole generation has been catechized by pop music to understand their emotions as truth and repression of these feelings as both unhealthy and a form of deceptive posturing.

Pop psychology has championed the cause of "listen to your heart." Anger management classes include verbalizing your anger to a present or absent object of your anger, venting one's wrath through shouting, or even physical rage. I once sat bewildered in a "pastor's" fraternal in which one pastor told the group that a suicide in his church had made him angry with God, and he felt it was healthy and healing to speak openly about his anger with God. The nodding and smiling heads around the table made me realize I was alone in my narrow theology of the book of Job.

Rare is the person today who doesn't see value in telling a group all his heart, in "admitting how you feel." Carl Roger's encounter groups have taken on myriad forms, from group therapy to market research focus groups, to church cell groups. Indeed, churches which don't give people the chance to "express themselves" must be repressive, authoritarian institutions where the male leadership is too insecure to allow for the healthy emotional expressions of its members' spiritual struggles. Emotional catharsis is taken to be some of the healthiest purgation available: let it all out.

Christian worship has been almost completely colonized by this approach. Because worship is rightly to be an act of sincere love for God, the Christian brought up in this culture begins to think that unless he has a strong sensation of his own feelings during worship, he must be less than sincere, perhaps falling into "mere ritual." So he pursues an intensity of feeling, closing his eyes to concentrate (usually scrunching up his face, too), hoping for the most emotive music and longing for a preacher who can pull on his heartstrings. Many Christians go looking for churches that have perfected the emotive approach, and enough churches see the market in creating a form of worship where everyone can feel his feelings. Of course, they won't call it "feeling your feelings;" they'll call it "connecting," "creating a worshipful atmosphere," "being authentic in our worship-expressions." But it amounts to using music, lights, and atmospherics, to give a generation whose primary art form is the movie an experience of escapist-like sensations during worship.

In reality, this is a fairly old idea which keeps getting a fresh coat of paint each year. French philosopher Rousseau taught that man in his natural state is at his best. The noble savage, uncorrupted by pretentious European civilization, is man at his most honest. So, too, is the man who does not manage and chasten his emotions, but lets them come out, raw and unfiltered. He is the sincere, authentic, Man of Passion.

Old-fashioned Romanticism, and its stepchild, sentimentalism, live upon these old lies. Feelings, like unrehearsed responses, represent our honest side; while feelings controlled and shaped represent inauthentic, phony people who just can't "be themselves."

Consider a contrasting view, by Roger Scruton:

> In a striking work published a century ago the Italian philosopher Benedetto Croce pointed to a radical distinction, as he saw it, between art properly so-called, and the pseudo-art designed to entertain, arouse or amuse.... [He was] right to believe that there is a great difference between the artistic treatment of a subject matter and the mere cultivation of effect...Genuine art also entertains us; but it does so by creating a distance between us and the scenes that it portrays: a distance sufficient to engender disinterested sympathy for the character, rather than vicarious emotions of our own.[2]

Scruton goes on to argue that true art works with imagination, representing ideas for our contemplation, and deliberately placing some distance between us and what we are contemplating. By doing so, it avoids evoking impulsive and visceral reactions and trains us, if we are patient with the process, to feel more carefully, and more circumspectly, about the object portrayed.

---

[2] Roger Scruton, *Beauty* (Oxford: Oxford University Press, 2009), 101.

AUTHENTIC

Manipulative art works with fantasy, trying to grip or excite us with a supposed portrayal of reality in which we get surrogate fulfilment of desires, substitute emotional experiences, purely for self-gratification.

To put it another way, art that lies takes shortcuts, shows us a mirror, and leads us to believe that hyped-up passions are evidence of how sincere and passionate we are, that our most superficial and immediate responses are the truest kinds. In reality, we are actually feeling *less*, like the hyper-emotional person who perpetually finds crisis and alarm in every situation. We don't envy such a person; we pity him, because we know that his intoxication with his own feelings blinds him to feel more deeply or carefully about the world. He is self-consciously hyper-emotional, and so he uses his drama as a perpetual shield from patiently thinking and feeling as she should.

Try telling the average person that he needs to have his emotions and sentiments properly trained, and he will think you are from outer space. Tell a man that his first and immediate emotional responses will usually be wrong, malformed, or inappropriate, and he will think you represent some Organization for the Suppression of Human Happiness. But the Christian understands the strange propensity of the human heart to deceive itself and realizes his feelings are some of the least reliable elements of his person.

AUTHENTICITY AND SINCERITY

While etymology doesn't determine the meaning of words, the proper meaning of *sincere* is not far from its root. A sincere man is one without pretence, without deception. Sincerity is very close to what the Bible calls integrity: wholeness, consistency. A man with integrity does not have a private life which contradicts his public claims. His character is not shot through with waxed over fatal flaws. A sincere man is a man with integrity, who seeks to be as much on the inside what he is on the outside.

Sincerity has nothing to do with formality or informality. One can be completely sincere and observe custom, ritual, or manners. Conversely, one could throw off all formality, be as casual as a surfer on Sunday, but remain a hypocrite, having different faces for different places.

Sincerity also has nothing to do with how public you make your inner or private world. Many of our private moments should remain just so. Instead of supporting the weird exhibitionism and voyeurism that much of social media encourages in all of us, we should foster a healthy privacy, without cultivating an unhealthy secrecy. Sincerity is not making a public confession where none was asked for, venting your frustration because you want to be "open and honest," or expecting some kind of therapeutic listen-'n-share group in the church.

AUTHENTIC

Sincerity has nothing to do with how sensate your feelings are to you. While worship must come from a sincere heart (1 Timothy 1:5; Matthew 6:1-18; 15:8), that really has nothing to do with how intensely you feel your feelings in worship. On a given Lord's Day, your physical condition, relative mental sharpness, or overall spiritual maturity may render your sense of your own affections less acute. That does not mean the worship was offered insincerely, or with the aim of impressing others, or to mask some monstrous sin.

Sincerity has nothing to do with how relaxed, casual, and familiar you feel. You may feel quite tense, nervous, or awkward, and be entirely sincere. Indeed, in circumstances or occasions of great moment, we would expect both sincerity *and* carefulness. It's true that awkwardness can tempt men to posture and act seriously, so as to fit in. It's equally true that casualness can tempt men to be flippant and profane, so as to fit in.

Sincerity has everything to do with *truth*. The sincere man wants the truth of reality, so he does not immerse himself in amusement. He wants truth in his words, so he learns to say what he means and mean what he says. He wants truth about God and man rightly symbolized, so he does not fear custom, tradition, or formality, but can penetrate their meaning and use them sincerely. He wants truth about himself, so he is able to acknowledge his failures, even among other believers (James 5:16), without polluting the minds of others with graphic descriptions of his every sin (Ephesians 5:12). He wants truth in his own affections, so he works on chastening and training his affections to love what he ought to love, in the way he ought to love it (Philippians 1:9-11), and on not giving place to every emotion that emanates from his heart.

In short, the sincere man is wrestling against the deceptiveness of his own nature, fighting man-pleasing, pride, hypocrisy, and narcissism. The very last thing he needs is to become intensely self-conscious of just how sincere he is (compared to all those fake, phony people out there, you know). That's like becoming proud of your achievements in humility.

Instead, he prays David's prayer for truth in the innermost man (Psalm 51:6). He repents of eyeservice. He seeks to love men, not please them. He does not "really want sincerity" as much as he sincerely wants reality.

2

AUTHORITY

The popular consciousness has knee-jerk reflexes when it comes to authority. Play the word-association game with the average person, show him the flashcard "authority," and ask him to blurt out the first word that comes to mind. I'll wager that if you repeat the experiment across thousands of subjects, you'll have a top-ten list pretty soon, and it'll sound something like "domineering," "exploitation," "dictatorship," "corrupt," "power-grab," "oppression," "bullying," "force," "abuse," "self-serving."

Of course, were you to do the same test with someone deeply saturated with Scripture and a Scriptural understanding of authority, the words would look completely different. Perhaps they would be something like: "order," "safety," "restraint," "grace," "delegation," "service," honor," "mediatorial," "protection," "roles."

Unfortunately, the average churchgoer has a fairly chronic (if not acute) case of secular culture-sickness. His cultural mentors have predominantly been movies, talk-show hosts, Facebook memes, and a few friends with similar influences. When this is shaping your cultural vocabulary, authority means something close to "the necessary evil of having someone in charge, who is usually a self-serving loser and needs to be watched extra carefully." Mix this in with some phrases he has heard ("the consent of the governed," "one man, one vote," "a government of the people, by the people, for the people") and what results is the idea that authority is really the permission that those following give to their leaders. From this mangled idea, churches are frequently accused of authoritarianism, "brain-washing," or spiritual abuse. Sometimes the charges are true; in some cases, even flawless leadership will be tarred with the same brush. Answering several questions may help us recover a biblical idea of authority.

First, what is authority? Where does it originate, and how does it propagate? Second, what is authority's purpose? If we understand its purpose, we will understand its lawful use, and, conversely, easily recognize its abuse. Third, how do we identify an authority, not only in church, but in wider society? Is there such a thing as expert opinion? Fourth, what does lawful authority look like in that community of self-denying servants, the Church? Democracy? Populism? How do churches incarnate and extend God's authority?

THE ORIGIN OF AUTHORITY

The English words *authority* and *author* come from the same Latin root, *auctor* – an originator. It is strange how far we've come from older ideas, where the concept of authority related to authoring, creating, and making. Today, authorities are guilty of being destroyers until proven innocent.

English etymology aside, Scripture, in its first chapter, makes the case for authority being creative. There, the God who brought order from chaos delegates a similar sub-creational role to Adam and Eve, saying, "Be fruitful and multiply; fill the earth and subdue it; have dominion over the fish of the sea, over the birds of the air, and over every living thing that moves on the earth" (Genesis 1:28). The Author calls on His image-bearers to author with Him. He authorizes them to exercise dominion over creation, subjugating it. Adam and Eve are to expand the Garden to encompass the Earth. They need authority to do so and have just received that delegated authority from God Himself. As Paul would say, "For there is no authority except from God, and the authorities that exist are appointed by God" (Romans 13:1).

Authority, then, is a gift from God. Order is superior to disorder, and God, the self-existent Authority delegates authority to man. Rightly used, it spreads the glory of God with loving subjugation. From the smallest acts of a humble vocation to the stately acts of princes and presidents, humans shaping creation are authorities. Furthermore, humans will not only order fields and streams, they are to order human life – which means exercising authority over one another. By creating Adam and Eve separately rather than simultaneously, God was symbolizing an authority structure for the home. So far, nothing is fallen or cursed in any of these concepts.

The problem began in Genesis 3. There Adam and Eve sought a new kind of authority. They were pleased to be King and Queen over the Earth, but Satan suggested they be *independent* kings and queens, rulers in their own right, determining what was good and evil for themselves. The act of eating the fruit, as mundane and simple as it was, represented a high-handed break from God's authority, a full-fledged declaration of independence from God, a revolt against the Author.

Every abuse of authority begins there. Every tyrannical king or president, every abusive husband, every cruel parent, every manipulative manager, every bullying pastor—indeed, every act of rebellion to God-given authority—is a ripple from the Tree. God's authority causes humans to flourish. All forms of its distortion, small or great, bring some kind of death.

Authority is *good*, and it is *permanent*. Authority is no necessary evil, nor is it a temporary arrangement. God will always rule, and He will always mediate that rule. The imperfections and evils of authority will pass away with sin, sorrow, and death, but authority will endure forever.

AUTHORITY

AUTHORITY AND AUTHORITARIANISM

When authority is usually discussed, about three sentences later, the word *authoritarian* will make its entrance. In fact, for some, authority is authoritarian – there is no other kind. Recovering the mangled word *authority* from all the thought-debris that has been hurled at it requires distinguishing it from authoritarianism. I'm not sure whether dictionaries help or hurt the cause of clarification, but for what it's worth, Webster's has *authoritarian* as "of, relating to, or favoring blind submission to authority" and "of, relating to, or favoring a concentration of power in a leader or an elite not constitutionally responsible to the people." For "English language learners," Webster's defines *authoritarian* as "expecting or requiring people to obey rules or laws," which, unfortunately, implicates every parent, schoolteacher, policeman, and pastor on the planet in authoritarianism.

The slipperiness of these definitions becomes downright frictionless once it gets into popular usage. There, *authoritarian* can mean anything from dogmatism to bullying, from having a visible leadership structure to insisting upon "blind submission" to unaccountable authority. And as we know, when something can mean almost anything, it means almost nothing.

If we have a biblical idea of authority, then *authoritarianism* must represent some kind of deviation from that idea. As we have seen, authority is good, and authority is grounded in Someone who did not derive His authority from anyone outside of Himself. God is a "concentration of power not constitutionally responsible to the people," but this is hardly a bad thing. For that matter, sometimes God requires submission without giving us lengthy explanations of the purpose or rationale behind our obedience. If that constitutes "blind submission," then there's a good deal of it in biblical religion.

Clearly, we need another way of distinguishing *authoritarianism* from biblical authority. Perhaps *authoritarianism* could be rightly defined as "human authority which asserts itself as an end in itself." Genuinely authoritarian leadership would be the kind that is more conscious of its position than of the direction it wishes to point others to, more aware of its status than its function. Authoritarian leadership mistakes the means (authority) for the end – which ought to be the glory of God and the good of our neighbor.

Having said that, discerning when authority has become authoritarian requires a prudent and sober judgment. It is not necessarily authoritarian to

- assert authority to accomplish God-glorifying goals;
- have explicit authority structures and teach the importance of submission;

- require submission and enforce it against the will of another (e.g., child discipline or church discipline);
- defend one's authority against rebellion or divisive people (e.g., the book of 2 Corinthians).

Every Christian parent, pastor, manager, or governor has to do every one of those four things at some point. Almost always, the accusation of authoritarianism will follow. But the humble leader must accept those calumnies as part of leading in a fallen world. He may be tempted to abdicate his role or back away when such accusations come, fearing that the appearance of authoritarianism is enough to mar his blamelessness. But this would actually be honoring his own reputation above the glory of God. It would be to cede ground to those who hate authority itself, not merely authoritarianism.

He may also be tempted to respond to such attacks or rebellion by furiously defending his role as leader and resorting to strong-arm tactics, intimidation, power-plays, or manipulation. Such fleshly behavior turns what was a false accusation into a true one. It plays into the hands of the scoffers who begin with lies and wait to see if they will materialize into truths.

He must accept that even the humblest leaders will be accused of self-promotion. "They gathered together against Moses and Aaron, and said to them, 'You take too much upon yourselves, for all the congregation is holy, every one of them, and the LORD is among them. Why then do you exalt yourselves above the assembly of the LORD?'" (Numbers 16:3).

A faithful leader's goal is to lead people to where God wants them, using God's methods, and seeking to display God's character. He need not defend himself against every fool, but he should explain authority and submission to those who have ears to hear. When God's church is in danger, he should defend the office of authority, even if it appears he is defending his own name. He should stay the course, outlast the rebels, disciple the teachable, and let the implacable implode on their own.

It is the easiest cheap shot to make: when authority acts like authority, accuse it of being authoritarian. But those under God's authority see through this. "Evil men do not understand justice, but those who seek the LORD understand all" (Proverbs 28:5).

WHO MADE YOU THE AUTHORITY?

The explosion of information on the web has made the idea of authoritative information almost a thing of the past. A CGI-Enhanced YouTube video about the non-existence of the South Pole is as accessible as the online *Encyclopedia Britannica*'s information on Antarctica. The crowd-edited Wikipedia is found as easily (or more so) than a peer-reviewed journal. The Internet has not only granted full democracy to all ideas, it has also tended to flatten out all judgment and scrap a sense of hierarchy of trustworthiness. No longer do canons of received knowledge exist in hard-bound Oxford or Cambridge Press volumes. No longer do scholars carry the weight of authority they once did in the popular mind. If a video has garnered three million views, it may just be true.

The democracy of ideas is simultaneously the pooling of ignorance. As computer scientist Robert Wilensky supposedly said in a speech, 'We used to think that a million monkeys typing away at a million keyboards could produce the works of Shakespeare. Now, thanks to the Internet, we know this is not the case.'"

For many, this democracy is seen as a good thing. After all, canonized error is harder to overturn than the slander and hear-say of the gossip-rags. Further, doesn't the whistle-blowing potential of the web keep people honest? Any man with a phone can now publish to a worldwide audience, and all strongholds of secrets are vulnerable. Ideas which would previously have been actively suppressed or dismissed by the large publishing houses can now see the light of day.

Benefits exist, to be sure. Hide-bound ideologies like Darwinism or liberal progressivism meet their match on the web. Like-minded people meet, though separated by oceans. False teachers and false teaching can be called out as soon as they record. Every idea is exposed to challenge through this technology.

On balance though, one wonders if the negatives outweigh the positives. It is the very cacophony of ideas, and the absence of some filter to discard and retain ideas, that tends to destroy any real sense of judgment in most people. People either grant authority to people and ideas that they ought not, or they become intensely cynical about anyone being an authority. Overwhelmed with ideas and competing authorities, the average person simply sets himself up as the authority, deciding eclectically what he deems plausible.

Witness the obsession with *fake news*. Is fake news alternative media? Is it news that does not support the agenda of the Broadcasting Magnates? Is it the news the Broadcasting Magnates disseminate? Who gets to decide? How do we decide? Or consider conspiracy theories. In the world of the Truthers, a conspiracy theory is true precisely because most people think it isn't. It is considered factual because *They* deny it. Every denial, or evidence to the contrary, finds an explanation that supports the Conspiracy Theory narrative.

What this amounts to is a crisis of authority. Who can be trusted? When criteria of judging knowledge to be authoritative have disappeared, when human authorities no longer exist, there is no good reason not to take seriously

AUTHORITY

YouTube discussions of the existence of mermaids, accounts of teleportation to Mars, or evidence of time travelers in old photographs.

But discerning who is an authority is exactly where things begin to fall down. We find ourselves in a kind of catch-22: authorities will give us the right kind of knowledge, but we need the right kind of knowledge to spot the genuine authorities from the self-appointed posers. Experts help us to discern the issues, but we first need to discern who the experts are. On what basis should I trust a professor's word over Wikipedia's? On what basis should I listen to one pastor and not another? On what basis should I trust one book over another?

This is where the value of tradition comes in. Whether it is an intellectual, cultural, or religious tradition, it reflects the process of elimination and assimilation that people do over centuries. Human beings were not meant to do on an individual level in a moment what is meant to happen on the scale of entire cultures over hundreds of years: evaluate meaning, recognize authorities, and deliver a consensus. Of course, we must each make judgments, and trust certain voices, but we were meant to do so with the backing of tradition. Within a culture, judgments are passed on from one generation to another. People who have spoken well on an issue are pointed to, and younger consciences are formed as they are exposed to these judgments. People growing up within the bounds of a tradition had the safety of hundreds of years of judgments from which to learn. If your father's father's father said it was good, useful, dangerous, healthy, true, or false, there was good reason to listen. When we don't know, we must trust our betters. In a tradition, we knew who our betters were.

Certainly, tradition can be a great evil if it hands down false religion, poor judgments or liars held up as paragons of virtue. But most cultures have experienced some common grace and, therefore, some truth. Few traditions are completely useless. Cultures most exposed to the special grace of the gospel usually have (or had) more evidence of helpful judgments handed down.

What we face now is every man adrift on a sea of opinion, cut loose from the Western cultural and intellectual tradition, cut loose from the Christian worship tradition, with gales of opinions battering each pathetic raft that each person is on. We are back to the book of Judges. Within this storm, we nevertheless have to (and do) choose whom we will trust. Whether the person is living or dead, we should consider three suggestions for evaluating his or her trustworthiness, and therefore, his or her authority. We'll consider these next.

AUTHORITY

IDENTIFYING AUTHORITIES

Within the avalanche of information coming at us, how do we identify true authorities in any domain of knowledge? How do we judge the anonymous YouTube channel, the self-proclaimed discernment ministry, the mega-church pastor, or the well-known author? We need something more than merely an intuitive feeling that a person "makes sense," or "seems to know what he's talking about." All false teachers do, or they wouldn't gain a following. Nor can we trust that we have some remarkable internal common-sense. Everyone thinks of himself as a pretty shrewd fellow, while the Bible unflatteringly calls the lot of us *sheep*. What follows is some suggested methods to wade through the morass.

1. In the case of living teachers of Christian virtue, does the person you trust exemplify the kind of life you are to follow? Is he an example of true Christian piety (Hebrews 13:7)?
2. Does the person you trust submit to a tradition himself? In the case of a Bible teacher, he must be able to defend his position using Scripture, sound reason, and a proven theological method. Something similar holds for a teacher in any other domain, be it science, history, economics, or human behavior. Can you evaluate his teaching against anything in the past? Does he seem to translate

and pass on what has been tried and tested in the past, or is he boasting in his novelty and creativity? The saying is mostly valid: *what's entirely new is seldom entirely true, and what's entirely true is seldom entirely new.*

3. Does the person you trust exemplify right thinking? Does he display good reason, sound judgment, unprejudiced evaluations, and fair-minded attitudes? This third qualification carries the catch-22 of "it takes one to know one," so we need to discipline ourselves in the canons of right thought to be able to see it in another.

When we choose to trust a person as some kind of expert in a particular domain of knowledge, we ought not to do so simply because the person seems to have such knowledge in great quantity. There is little skill in accumulating vast amounts of knowledge and only marginally more in impressing others with the size of that knowledge. What counts when it comes to the pursuit of truth is whether a person demonstrates the ability to think. Right thinking is not vast recall, or enormous powers of regurgitation. Right thinking has to do with how knowledge is assimilated, analyzed, and judged. People are led astray because they are mesmerized by the sound 'n fury of a lot of facts and figures. "If someone can

AUTHORITY

remember that much, they must be clever enough to follow."

Mortimer Adler wrote a very important and useful book for the development of right thinking, called *How to Read a Book*.[1] What follows is an abridged summary of his guidelines for the right assimilation of information, followed by the correct understanding of its meaning and of its significance.

- Come to terms with an author by understanding what the important words are in his work and what he means by them.
- Having done so, discover the key propositions, premises and conclusions contained in the work.
- From these, understand the author's argument. Observe if his argument is deductive or inductive. Observe what he assumed. Observe what he says can be proved, what need not be proved and what is self-evident.
- Consider what his solutions are.
- At this point, the work of criticizing the contents of the book takes over. Critical judgment will say *I agree, I disagree,* or *I suspend judgment* with good reasons for doing so. Critical judgment can only be

---

[1] Mortimer Adler and Charles Van Doren, *How to Read a Book* (New York, NY: Simon and Schuster, 1972).

done when you can state the author's argument in terms he would agree with.

To judge critically is to acknowledge your emotion, make your assumptions explicit and attempt impartiality. The disagreement will not be mere opinion; it will give reasons for the disagreement without being contentious.

There are three ways of disagreeing rationally with an author, stated as responses to the author:

1. "You are uninformed" – the author lacks relevant knowledge.
2. "You are misinformed" – the author makes assertions contrary to the facts.
3. "You are illogical" – the author reasons poorly or fallaciously.

A fourth way exists, which is really a way of suspending judgment. It is to say, "Your analysis is incomplete," which is to say that the author has not solved all the problems or did not see the ramifications and implications of his ideas, or failed to make relevant distinctions, or failed to make as good a use of materials as possible.

Once we have begun to grasp and practice these ways of handling knowledge, we are better off in two ways. First, we are able to better handle the knowledge coming at us from every side. If a book, or website or video fails the tests of right thinking, and does so again and again, there is no reason to trust its analysis or to place much stock in it. Second, we are better able to evaluate the teachers of knowledge themselves. A person who consistently commits fatal errors of logic, whose sources are erroneous, or who mishandles his materials, disqualifies himself from our consideration of him as an expert. No matter the domain of knowledge, we want to hear from people who think properly when they handle that knowledge.

It might seem that we are a long way from plain biblical discernment when we speak of right thinking, but that is because we have imbibed a form of thinking which divorces the God-glorifying task of good thinking from the God-glorifying task of biblical interpretation. If we think well, we are better able to spot teachers who handle the text of Scripture properly. If we think well, we will consult the right people on various areas of human knowledge and distinguish the authorities from the posers.

YOU ELITIST, YOU

Since this book has dealt with "mangled" words such as *tolerance, freedom,* and *authority,* I was tempted to include *elitism* among them. Elitism, though, is really a misused word inseparable from the word *authority.* When the meaning of authority is mangled, be sure that a sorely maimed and deformed version of the meaning of elitism will make a showing.

This word makes its appearance in some Christian circles whenever a discussion of art, taste, or critical judgment comes up. That is, *elitism* does not rear its head when the discussion is over a simple prescription or prohibition from Scripture. There, Christians are happy to ping-pong proof texts at one another. Should the conversation require some extra-biblical information from experts, say from a musical composer, or a professor of literature, or a cultural critic, suddenly many Christians get uncomfortable and feel that the elitist camel is poking its nose into the tent. They might not think of it this way, but they are really struggling with the idea of authority and doing so in two ways.

First, they feel that an appeal to any information outside of Scripture is a subversion of the authority of Scripture. They wish Scripture and Scripture alone to settle every debate. While this desire is commendable, it is neither the meaning of *sola Scriptura*, nor is it the meaning of the doctrine of Scripture's sufficiency. *Sola Scriptura* teaches that Scripture is the final authority. What God says has the final say and overrules all other opinions. But *sola Scriptura* does not mean no other authorities exist in the world. The world is full of authorities on politics, medicine, history, nutrition, economics, art, the natural sciences and so on. *Sola Scriptura* simply means that none of these authorities has equal authority with Scripture. Once these authorities have spoken, their views must be submitted to the final bar of God's Word. Scripture gets to overrule any and all of them. That is not the same as saying we may safely ignore these authorities and depend on Scripture to answer every question. That attitude is not *sola Scriptura*, it is what is known as *nuda Scriptura* – naked texts expected to function apart from any other knowledge of the world around us.

The Bible was never meant to deal with every branch of human knowledge or to speak expertly on every topic. It provides commands and principles that cover all that we need for life and godliness. This is its sufficiency. But these principles, in order to find application in our lives, most often require that we gather knowledge from the created order and submit it to the God-breathed timeless principles of God's Word. For example, to obey Romans 13:1–4, I need to learn the laws of the land, and Scripture doesn't give those to me. To avoid enslavement to something (1 Corinthians 6:12), I need to find out what substances or activities are addictive, and Scripture does not identify these for me. Scripture is sufficient to thoroughly equip us, but no one expects Scripture to tell us which foods are healthy, which fashions are immodest, which technologies are edifying. Most of our knowledge will come from outside the Bible. All our extra-biblical knowledge must submit to the grid of Scripture to be properly understood, and any knowledge that Scripture explicitly contradicts is false. But Scripture is sufficient not in the sense that it exists to be the sum total of necessary knowledge for life. It is sufficient in that its prescriptions, principles, and wisdom, when used to judge and evaluate all other gathered knowledge, gives us all we need to live a life glorifying to God.

Second, even among those Christians who are willing to accept expert extra-biblical opinion when it comes to medicine, economics, or science, there exists a deep suspicion of any expert opinion regarding music, poetry, literature, or the arts. Supposedly this is simply too arcane, too subjective, and perhaps even too mystical for any opinion to be held as more authoritative than another. And should one quote or refer to those whose vocation is to understand the fine arts, i.e., critics, it won't be long before the word *elitism* is thrown in.

Elitism, properly defined, is rule or influence by an elite. *Elite*, in turn, refers to a class of people superior to others in rank, ability or power. In a democratic age, the idea that elites exist is both acknowledged and resented. Perhaps it is most strongly resented in the evangelical church, which since at least the 19th century, has become strongly populist.

Populism assumes that all that is true and good and necessary to life can be understood equally by all and accessed or perceived immediately, without specialized training or instruction. To a populist, what God wants us to know is what is absolutely necessary to know, and what is absolutely necessary to know must therefore be uncomplicated, immediately accessible, and transparently practical. Recourse is made to texts about receiving the kingdom as a little child, and this is supposed to end the discussion. Consequently, populism views higher learning with suspicion. Populism views consulting experts with suspicion. Populism views advanced studies with suspicion. Populism views tradition with suspicion. Populism views authority with suspicion. Populism views intellectuals with suspicion. The upshot is a roll-your-own-at-home Christianity, where sincerity and an open Bible will supply all we need.

There are two responses to populism. One is to rightly understand the priesthood of the believer alongside the doctrine of vocation. The second is to understand the role of critical judgments. We'll consider these next.

AUTHORITY, SOUL COMPETENCE, AND VOCATION

Soul competence and the priesthood of the believer are two sides of one doctrine that Baptists cherish. Indeed, they make up part of the matrix known as the Baptist distinctives. Soul competence teaches that individual Spiritindwelt believers can read and understand Scripture for themselves, using the means He has given. The priesthood of the believer means that every individual believer in Christ can approach God directly through the High Priestly work of Christ. Whether we are dealing with the Word or prayer, a New Testament believer is not dependent on human intermediaries between himself and God. The work of salvation is so thorough a work that if a Christian makes right use of the Spirit's appointed means, he lacks nothing to worship God directly.

Unfortunately, these doctrines are easily misunderstood or misapplied. When populism is part of the cultural air we breathe, such misunderstandings become almost inevitable. The most infantile of these misunderstandings is the person who opts for "home-church," or Internet-church, or some other excuse to be anti-ecclesiological and reject authority. Here the person dismisses the need for corporate worship, instruction by pastors, service to the body, or shared life in Christ, all in the name of the believer's priesthood. Such abuses of the doctrine are easily spotted and easily refuted.

A more subtle form of this misunderstanding is the believer who thinks that if God has granted direct access to His presence and an ability to understand Scripture, then anything worth knowing is within the immediate intellectual grasp of every believer. The logic is arguing from the apparently greater to the apparently lesser: if knowing the greatest thing – the Gospel – is open to even a little child, then there cannot be lesser things worth knowing which are harder to understand. Emerging from this attitude will be the populist suspicion of philosophy, of theology, of disciplines of thought, of advanced studies, of intellectuals and of academia in general.

The mistake the populist imports into his theological method is to assume that there is a proportional relationship between clarity and importance: the more important something is, the clearer it must be, and the less important, the more difficult it may be to understand. Were we to consistently embrace this view, we would have to conclude that the doctrines of the Trinity, hypostatic union, and election are of minor importance due to their difficulty. In reality, crucial doctrine is often enough not simple or even perspicuous.

The correct approach is to recognize that nearly everything worth knowing has multiple levels of deepening complexity and sophistication. A five-year-old can grasp substitution in the Gospel, while doctors in theology may give themselves to decades of studying its meaning. These levels of complexity apply whether we are speaking of biblical doctrines, mathematics, the natural sciences, history, music, the arts, or any area of knowledge in God's created order. This naturally invites the question, "But how much of this complexity do we *need* to know?"

God has so made the world and limited man that we each need to specialize in some domain of human life. We need some to give themselves to knowing human physiology so as to become experts in medicine and healing. We need some to give themselves to the physics of motion so as to become engineers. We need some to give themselves to understanding the market so as to become experts in economics. And we need some to give themselves to the study of music, painting, poetry, literature, and architecture, so as to become experts in the arts. No one can master all the realms of knowledge in the short lifespan appointed to us. It is one of God's mercies to the world: forcing interdependence, trade, and learning.

This is the doctrine of vocation. God calls and equips humans to function well in some area of human life, to bring order and meaning to some section of the created order (1 Corinthians 7:20–21). Not only so, but God invests His world with meanings, laws, and "secrets," which become the duty of man to learn, master and teach others (Proverbs 25:2).

The answer to the question, "How much of this complexity do we need to know?" is answered by the doctrine of vocation. If you are a doctor, you need to be an expert on health since that is your calling. If you are not a doctor, you need to know enough about health to stay reasonably healthy, and you need to know when to consult a medical expert. We don't sneer at doctors and call them elitists; we are thankful that when our basic competence in health and medicine can take us no further, there are experts to do just that. The same is true for engineering, financial planning, and software development. Now buckle your seatbelt: the same is true for theology, music, poetry, and literature.

Soul competence and the priesthood of the believer does not remove the need for pastors, nor for professional theologians. Similarly, the fact that every individual Christian can lift his or her voice in sincere praise does not remove the need for art critics, composers, or poets.

In the end, I have never met a consistent populist. I have never met the man who was willing to do surgery on himself, act as a lawyer for every one of his contractual agreements, and write his own software. He is usually selectively populist— sneering at theologians, composers, critics, and pastors, but happy to accept expert opinion in other areas of his life. If he would accept the doctrine of vocation, he could reconcile the priesthood of the believer and soul competence with the authority of expert opinion, even in matters that touch the soul. He would see, in a word, that no one can know it all. It is an act of humility to accept your own limitations and learn from those called to be authorities in some domain of human knowledge.

CHRISTIANS AND CRITICAL JUDGMENTS

Most Christians are happy to accept the authority of expert opinion. What is instructive to note is which domains of knowledge they are comfortable to refer to experts, as opposed to those in which they actively oppose expert opinion. To paraphrase what I wrote to one commenter, Christians are happy to listen to experts when they are biologists or geologists, and the topic is creationism/evolution. Christians are happy to turn to experts when they are neurologists, and the topic is depression and the use of anti-depressants. The expert opinion that these men will bring, when submitting their findings to the principles of Scripture, is deemed helpful – and rightly so. For some reason, when the topic is the more critical judgments of art, the experts are disparagingly called "gatekeepers," or "elitists," who think their job is to "keep out the unwashed and allow in the pure."

Why is this so? I have no way of proving this, but I suspect many Christians have embraced the "double-story" view of truth. Immanuel Kant is really the central culprit here. He taught that human knowledge comes in two separate layers, or floors. The lower floor we might call "scientific" or rational knowledge. It's the kind of knowledge we can work out using mathematics, or measure with scientific experiments. The upper floor we might call "moral" or intuitive knowledge, and it refers to religious beliefs, morals, and judgments about beauty. Kant believed that only the lower story could be known with certainty, through empirical observation. The upper story, he felt, was "impossible to know, but morally necessary to suppose." What that translates to in the contemporary situation is the idea that science delivers hard facts, while art delivers neutral material which obtains only "personal" judgments, variable from subject to subject.

Christians seem to believe this. They believe we need experts to fight infection in the body, build airplanes, and program software because this kind of knowledge is, to them at least, entirely "objective." But determining if a song is sensual, if a poem's rhythm is comical, if a film is subversive to Christian affections is, to them, no longer a matter of collecting empirical facts and must, therefore, be "subjective," which, in their parlance, usually means "arbitrary in meaning." Of course, if this is so, an expert in these areas is not only contradictory (for how can one person's judgment be authoritative if no authoritative or universal judgment is possible?), it becomes preposterous—like having a color-inspector tell you if your interior decoration is lawful or not.

But Kant's dichotomy is open to challenge, and few strict Kantians exist anymore. What Christians need to embrace is the truth that while judgments about music and art are indeed of a different kind from those of math and science, *they are all still judgments*. All knowledge is a matter of judgment and interpretation, even the manipulation of numbers, or the direct observation of the universe. It is all performed by subjects, and, in that sense, all knowledge is "subjective." The difference between a judgment of art and one of science is not that one is exterior and the other interior, or that the one is discoverable while the other is mystically unknowable. The real difference is that aesthetic, moral, and religious knowledge is knowledge that pertains to persons, and so the judgment requires a more careful, critical judgment.

Ethical and aesthetical judgments are difficult. It is easier to work out the circumference of a circle than it is to determine how Christians smuggling Bibles into a country should deal with the border agents. Such an ethical judgment is hard, but not impossible. It calls for the combined thinking of many Christians on the topics of truthfulness, governmental authority, civil disobedience, conflicting obligations, and questions of greater goods and lesser evils. It's a critical judgment.

Judging art and beauty requires a similarly critical judgment. Such judgment requires a thoughtful examination of form and of the materials used in the art form. It requires knowledge of the symbols and metaphors within a culture. It usually requires historical knowledge, understanding the "conversation" that has taken place within the culture, so that it can place the work within that conversation. The critic, if he is doing is job, is not "forcing his preference" on us, nor is he "criticizing" the work, in the sense of tearing it down. He is explaining meaning to us, using his knowledge of the form, his knowledge of history, and his own sense of perception. He should not tell us what we could not, with the right tools, see ourselves; that is, he is not some kind of mediator, interpreting a language that no one else can understand. Nevertheless, he ought to possess a superior knowledge of art and enough experience and insight to help us see more and become better judges ourselves.

Certainly, we live in an era when we lack a living tradition, and we feel more cut off from art than most generations before us probably ever did. In this atmosphere, we need critics more than ever, while suspecting rightly that the wrong critics have more power to mislead than ever. The solution is not to retreat to Kantian notions of the impossibility of knowing beauty. The solution is to choose critics immersed in the Western and Christian tradition. Unless we believe moral, religious, and aesthetic judgments are all arbitrary, it is entirely permissible and indeed, necessary, to turn to authorities in these areas, to help shape our judgments.

3

CULTURE

Jackhammers are not the ideal tool for mixing cake batter. A mess will almost certainly be the result. Evangelical Christians using the word "culture" often remind one of a baker with a such a power tool. When some evangelicals begin writing or speaking on culture, one winces. A migraine is certainly on its way.

The word *culture*, in the hands of evangelicals is plasticine. It is verbal playdough and can be shaped nearly infinitely. What follows are some favorite forms they like to make:

1. Culture is "the stuff people do, and the way they are." This definition has the nifty distinction of including everything and excluding nothing. Everything is culture. Of course, when a word means everything, the disadvantage is that it simultaneously defines nothing.
2. Culture is race. Skin-color and, in some cases, home language, is equivalent to culture. For this reason, the church must be "multicultural," and multiculturalism is touted and celebrated by some

Christians, who should have committed Proverbs 17:28 to memory.
3. Culture is "the way of life" in a city or nation. Music, food, clothing, customs, and attitudes are put into the blender, and the puree that results is called "their culture."

But none of these will do. Culture cannot be everything for it to be a useful concept. Culture is definitely not the quasi-secular concept of race. Culture is not a collection of habits. When Christians think of culture in these terms, we can expect calamitous results.

If there is one word that Christians should be especially careful to define, it is *culture*. After all, culture is formative and determinative in every area that matters—worship, discipleship, evangelism, and missions. What and how you sing, how you present the Gospel, your idea of Christian devotion, and your approach to matters of conscience are all determined by your understanding of culture and how that understanding is worked out in life and ministry. Indeed, when we "export" Christianity in the form of global missions, our understanding of culture is tested at nearly every point. A gelatinous understanding of culture leads to embracing and endorsing what should be rebuked and importing and imposing what ought to be left at home.

CULTURE

But how many seminaries teach on culture in missiology, besides pointing out the obvious ("people will do things very differently where you're going")? How many apologetics classes teach the meaning of culture, and how it shapes presuppositions, instead of merely harping on about axiomatic presuppositions? How many pastoral theology classes explain what a Christian culture looks like, instead of merely talking knowingly about contextualization? How many church history classes are concerned with tracing the development and decline of Christian culture through the ages, instead of using it to produce hagiographies? One wonders how an idea so central to Christianity goes mostly undefined through years of ministerial training. And where there's a mist at the lectern, there will be a fog in the seats.

Does it matter? It may not matter if the average Christian cannot formally define culture properly. It does matter when his *idea* of culture is amorphous and secular. Such a Christian will lack a crucial element of the Christian life: discernment. Understanding culture is fundamental to understanding cultural phenomena, and it is cultural phenomena that we bump into all the time: music, language, dress, conventions, customs, technologies, foods, social structures, and ethical matters. When a Christian does not understand the meaning of these things, he cannot respond obediently to them. He cannot discern their meaning and their proper use, so he cannot be pleasing to God in the areas in which he lacks discernment. In sum, the Christian life is incarnated in culture, and a faulty view of culture will lead to errors in judgment, both major and minor.

For this reason, rescuing the word *culture* from its mangled form is no mere academic pursuit. It is how we obey God in the present world.

MORE THAN CREATION

If the word *culture* is to be useful, it must define something. It must name and describe a discrete phenomenon in the world. A useful definition must limit its subject, so that we could easily say what is *not* culture.

The problem with many definitions found in evangelical literature is that they seem to include everything. If everything in the created order is an instance of culture, then we may as well scrap the word and speak plainly of creation.

Culture is not the created order. Time, space, and matter are not culture, and Genesis 1 and 2 are not the account of God creating culture. Creation is used in creating culture, but it is not culture itself.

Culture is not the *world*, as the Bible variously uses the term to mean the created order, mankind, the age we are in, or the system of thought and habit that opposes God.

CULTURE

As Christians dependent upon Scripture for our understanding of reality, we face a real difficulty in defining culture precisely. Scripture does not contain the word. The English word *culture* is used in its modern sense from the 19th century on. We are then in the dilemma of either reading into Scripture a modern, but false construct, or of locating in Scripture a real phenomenon, one which Scripture names differently.

What Scripture does describe is what man does. Man is a meaning-making creature. He orders his world to incarnate and symbolize his understanding of the meaning of reality. In Genesis 1, God turns chaos into order. Man, made in God's image, is told to extend this work throughout the world, turning what is less ordered into something more ordered and meaningful. Humans do this because they are like God. They do not create as He creates, but they do take the raw unordered creation and shape it into systems of meaningful order. They do this not only to the physical world, but to the life of the mind, to matters both intellectual and moral.

This phenomenon is culture-making. Humans make cultures. A culture grows out of a *cultus* (religion). The people share the same vision of what is behind and beyond this world. They agree on what the world is, on what man is, and on what deities are ruling over it all. They agree on the moral order that should govern life. In short, a culture incarnates and expresses a religion. Everything in a culture is affected by the religion: art, science, jurisprudence, economics, politics, and social etiquette. Religion is the lens through which all of life is viewed and understood. The group of people who share a location and share this religion then shape their world so as to cultivate their idea of reality.

The account of the Tower of Babel reveals a time when mankind had one culture, spoke one language, and was intent on symbolizing their one idolatrous religion with a Tower. God's scattering of the nations was both judgment and mercy. In the diversifying of language (and therefore of culture), God "determined their pre-appointed times and the boundaries of their dwellings, so that they should seek the Lord, in the hope that they might grope for Him and find Him, though He is not far from each one of us" (Acts 17:26-27). The call of Abram is the beginning of God creating a culture for Himself, from which will come the redemption of all other cultures.

Cultures are humanly created systems of meaning. They are systems of meaning growing out of a *cultus*, that in their turn *cultivate* a shared sentiment about reality.

NOT RACE

Scripture does not define the word *culture*, but it certainly describes the phenomenon of culture-making. Humans are meaning-making creatures who fashion their world after their values, religions, and worldviews.

The Bible also describes the behavior or way of life that comes from a certain culture. The Greek word *anastrophe* is translated *conduct*, or way of life. In contrast to those who define culture as "everything people do" the biblical writers see one's *anastrophe* as rooted in one's religion. That is, idolatry and false systems produce one kind of anastrophe, whereas Christianity is supposed to produce another.

> As obedient children, not conforming yourselves to the former lusts, as in your ignorance; but as He who called you is holy, you also be holy in all your conduct [anastrophe], because it is written, "Be holy, for I am holy." And if you call on the Father, who without partiality judges according to each one's work, conduct [anastrophe—verb form] yourselves throughout the time of your stay here in fear; knowing that you were not redeemed with corruptible things, like silver or gold, from your aimless conduct [anastrophe] received by tradition from your fathers, but with the precious blood of Christ, as of a lamb without blemish and without spot. (1 Peter 1:14-19)

Peter contrasts one form of culture with another. One was received by tradition (which is simply a culture stretched over time); the other is shaped by the new life in Christ.

Here we see the tragic misstep of equating culture with race. For if culture and race are synonymous, no culture can be critiqued. One would then be judging the value of a people based upon skin color, which is racism proper.

Scripture does not critique people based upon their *ethnos* (ethnicity). It does, however, critique their *anastrophe*, which is to say, their culture. If the culture of a people has produced immorality, idolatry, or perversions, Scripture condemns the culture. In condemning the culture, it is condemning the belief-system that created that behavior.

One sees the sad result of equating race and culture in South Africa. Here, untaught believers will still refer to "my culture" as a contrast to another believer's "culture." You will routinely hear people say that missionaries brought "their culture" and imposed it upon Africa. Some dear black believers are desperately trying to discover some pristine form of "black Christian culture" untouched by Western hands. Believers speak of certain ways of worship as belonging to one culture (by which they mean *ethnicity*) as opposed to another.

Now I, for one, rejoice in the diversity of our country and of my local church. I love the many colors that look back at me on a Sunday morning. I enjoy being called "Mfundisi" (teacher) by some of the members. I enjoy tasting, hearing, and seeing the mix of foods, languages, and social customs that mingle in our local church. A multiethnic church is a joy. Racism is an evil, and I will, as the occasion suggests, write and preach against racism as a sin.

But our church is not "multicultural." That would be equivalent to saying, it is "multi-anastrophal," or "multi-religious." No, in the biblical sense, our church is monocultural. We love and honor Christ. With Scripture as our final authority, it shapes the loves, beliefs, and behavior of those who are part of our church. However much melatonin the skin of the various members contain, however many of our country's eleven national languages (yes, eleven!) they speak, however different some of our social customs may be, we are actually bound and shaped by one culture: Christian culture.

I recognize speaking of "Christian culture" raises several other questions. What place is there for differing expressions of music or art in this supposed Christian culture? Has Christian culture existed in the past, and what did it look like? What if one ethnic group has dominated in historic Christian culture? What element of missions was pure ethnic preference, and what was true Christian culture? Should modern missionaries attempt to leave the cultures they find in as pristine a state as possible? We will attempt to deal with these questions as we rehabilitate this mangled word.

CHRISTIAN CULTURE IN CHURCH HISTORY

A common error in the study of church history is to seek to find a version of one's present branch of Christianity in the past. Since Christian doctrine and practice develop over the centuries, trying to find oneself in church history is like trying to find out how people in Shakespeare's era texted one another or trying to understand what Edward II's position on globalism was. You won't find covenant theology or dispensationalism (in the self-conscious, self-identified form) before the 17th century, cessationism (as a reaction to Pentecostalism) before the twentieth, or Baptists who hold to justification by faith before the 16th. There are no self-conscious, self-identified credobaptist, compatibilist, cessationist, creationist, complementarian, and chiliast believers like me more than a hundred years ago. This doesn't mean those positions are not biblical or did not exist in church history; it simply means the faith once delivered to the saints has been progressively understood by the saints. I won't find in the early church a theological understanding that took 2000 years to develop.

Similarly, if it is an error to imagine some ancient version of one's own church or denomination, it is equally an error to imagine that somewhere in history there existed a pristine and nearly perfect form of Christianity. The perfect group chosen usually depends upon the sympathies of the speaker: some of the Reformed imagine it was

Calvin's Geneva; certain Methodists picture the revivals under Wesley; similarly, some Baptists think that the Metropolitan Tabernacle under Spurgeon was almost the Millennium; some anti-Calvinists pin their hopes on some pre-Reformation groups, such as the Waldenses; others romanticize the Middle Ages. But all of these had points of doctrine, practice and worship that were less than perfect and revealed a church still in development. No straight line from the apostles to the present day exists.

Recognizing these two errors might lead us to a faulty conclusion: the notion that there has never been an instance of Christian culture. To agree that no perfect example of Christianity exists in the past is not to assert that Christian culture has never existed. Quite the contrary.

This error comes from trying to judge or think about Christian culture in the abstract, rather than in the form of cultural phenomena and cultural artifacts. Concrete cultural artifacts produced by Christians exist in abundance: songs, paintings, poems, buildings, treatises, histories, sermons, buildings, customs, and the like. Wherever Christianity has taken hold of the majority of a population in one place, it will soon be seen shaping the sagas, political arrangements, clothing, technologies, and even language itself. If a culture is a religion externalized, then wherever Christianity becomes dominant, cultural forms representing that worldview will appear.

At what point can we say a form of Christian culture was in a certain place, for a certain time? It depends on how dominant Christianity became, how long its dominance held, and how healthy the form of Christianity was that was known and practiced. But that it has done so in many times and places is beyond dispute.

A second error follows the first. In trying to imagine a Christian culture in the abstract, a person assumes its incarnation will look identical in every instance. When he finds that Christians of varying ethnicities developed different forms of music, architecture, and literature, he wrongly concludes that one cannot speak about Christian culture at all. To him, the differences seem to eliminate any unifying principle.

What our interlocutor misses is glaring. The most interesting thing about comparing different cultural artifacts from different Christian communities is not that they are different, it is how similar they are. Indeed, while no one expects Armenian and Chinese Christianity to be identical, what is fascinating is to find equivalence in cultural forms between Christians separated by thousands of miles or hundreds of years.

Equivalence is the proper word. When two forms are equivalent between two groups, they may not share the same shape or incarnation, but they carry the same meaning in their respective communities. They are like the same idea in different languages. Two reverent Christian communities will produce different cultural artifacts, but they will both have words for "reverence," both have postures for reverence, both have combinations of musical notes for reverence. Often enough, a visitor from the one will be able to broadly decode the reverential tone of a form in the other. All this speaks of *equivalence* between two different instances of Christian culture.

Church history reveals something far more interesting than a pristine Christian culture in one time and place; it reveals very different ethnicities, languages, and traditions that often enough produced artifacts that have passed into common use by Christians around the world. The equivalence was sufficient to have "catholic" value. The "leaven" of Christianity leavened the whole cultural lump of particular peoples and particular times and so produced different Christian cultures.

Where we find strong equivalences in forms and artifacts between folk cultures, since they shared Christianity, we find something like Christian culture in its most general and extensive sense. These equivalences make up a universal, two-thousand-year-old tradition of orthodoxy, orthopraxy, and orthopathy. And a tradition is simply a culture stretched over time.

"WE DON'T WANT YOUR WHITE MAN RELIGION"

In Africa, particularly where black nationalist sentiments arise, it is not uncommon to hear these words thrown around in conversation. Similarly, half-formed sentiments are uttered about missionaries who replaced the harmonious earth-religion of the peaceful indigenous people with their foreign religion to steal their land and subjugate them.

The saddest irony of these assertions being made is that these sentiments are not even African. They were really birthed by Europeans influenced by the Enlightenment (particularly Rousseau and his "noble savage" idea). Those most vociferously calling for a pure African religious identity purged of the infection of European missionaries are unwittingly busy borrowing from other, less honorable, Europeans.

What is more important is whether there is any truth to these accusations. First, was the missionary movement of Christianity merely a disguised land-grab? Second, didn't missionaries simply have their own culture, which they then imposed upon the indigenous people, unnecessarily displacing perfectly healthy cultural patterns?

Land-grabs in the name of religion are a painful and evil part of history. No defense of these can be offered, except that Jesus said his servants were not to fight for an earthly kingdom (John 18:36). When it was done, it was certainly not an act of obedience to Christ or a legitimate part of missions. Missionaries are to plant churches, not conquer land. Too often, opportunistic politicians piggybacked upon the genuine mission-work of missionaries (think Cecil John Rhodes using David Livingstone's work).

The second question suffers from a misunderstanding of the meaning of *culture*. Did the missionaries have "their own culture?" Of course they did, as do we all. But if a culture is the incarnation of a religion, a religion externalized, then to the degree that those missionaries were allegiant to biblical Christianity, and to the degree that they had been shaped and formed by healthier forms of Christianity, their culture would have been a valid expression of Christian ideas.

The fact that these particular Christian missionaries were Caucasian is beside the point. What matters is if Christianity had come to dominate the worldview of the region in which they grew up. As it turns out, Christianity, in the broadest, trinitarian sense, came to dominate Europe for 1000 years. Pagan, warlike, and superstitious people in Europe were progressively transformed into the people that produced Milton, the Chartres Cathedral, the Magna Carta, Shakespearian Sonnets, and Bach. It had nothing to do with the amount of melanin in the skin and everything to do with what worldview came to dominate.

In God's providence, Christianity's center moved through the centuries from the Middle East, to Asia

Minor, to North Africa, to Western Europe, and to North America. During the era of the modern missionary movement (1750s onwards), Christianity was strongest in Europe and North America. Wherever it remained, it shaped those people and their entire culture—not perfectly, nor completely, but significantly. When Christians left their homelands to take the Gospel somewhere else, they were necessarily bringing the Gospel and their particular Christian culture to a people largely or totally bereft of it.

That same providence which centered Christianity in certain regions during certain eras also allowed that some continents or lands to experience centuries of what Romans 1 describes: the devolution that idolatry brings. That does not mean that no common grace existed in those places: Acts 14:17 says that it did. But to the degree that cultures were formed around animism, sun-worship, or some other form of idolatry, is the degree to which we would expect the image of God in them to have been further defaced and marred. We would expect their cultures, as the missionaries found them, to be externalizations of idolatry, as pre-Christian European culture certainly was.

Were those missionaries coming to a non-Christian culture then supposed to present a "culturally-neutral" Christianity to the people they evangelized? Such a thing is difficult to even conceptualize, let alone practice. A missionary not only teaches ideas, he teaches the people to sing, to speak a certain way, to dress, to worship, to obey

God in all of life, and so on. He must, and necessarily will, shape the culture of the people he evangelizes.

He must start somewhere and present the newly converted people some cultural forms, especially if the indigenous ones he finds present are irredeemably idolatrous in meaning. (This is worth exploring further, and we'll do so in the next section.)

As an example, we might reference Robert Moffat in southern Africa, who not only translated the Bible into Tswana, but also many hymns. He produced the first Tswana hymnbook and the first original hymn in Tswana.

Is this imposing "white culture" upon "black culture?" No; it is presenting translated forms of a Christian culture that grew up in Europe to an infant Christian culture in another place. As these people imbibe Christianity, and it shapes them for generations, they will eventually speak in their own voice. But you must learn to walk before you can sprint, and one of the healthier things that a newborn Christian culture can do is hear the songs, histories, poems, sermons, and biographies of the church universal. Avoiding these cultural forms in the name of ethnic nationalism is simply pride and will not produce a pure "African" or "Asian" Christianity. It will likely produce another syncretized Christianity with idolatrous ideas mixed in with Christianity. The only way to see the idolatry in your own culture is to step away from it by being exposed to the culture of historic Christianity, which has spanned five continents and two thousand years.

It took more than a millennium of Christian ideas in Europe to produce a Bach. We may still be centuries away from an African Bach or a Chinese Notre Dame or a Polynesian Watts. But that is a function of time, not of skin color. In many ways, Christianity has taken hold in Africa, South America, and south-east Asia a lot faster than it did in Europe. True, often the Christianity is a mile wide and an inch deep. Often, pop culture is secularizing the Christianity that emerges. But it remains to be seen how true Christianity will leaven the cultural lump in Africa, Asia, and South America.

Will Europeans and North Americans eventually be saying to missionaries from Africa, "We don't want your black man religion?" Perhaps it will sadly be the case. For man, ever seeking justification for his rebellion against God, finds great convenience in the excuse that the Gospel must be untrue because it was brought to him by people from a foreign nation, who had it before he did.

MISSIONARIES AND CULTURE

Missionaries do their work in a perilous environment. Such has been the rise of ideas such as "multiculturalism" that many missionaries now go by a different title: *aid-workers, social-workers, educators,* or even *consultants.*

CULTURE

Opting for different titles is understandable. In the popular imagination, *missionary* is increasingly synonymous with colonialist, imperialist, or patronizing religious types "forcing" their fundamentalist notions of exclusive paths to God.

For the missionaries on the ground, the bigger challenge is not how unbelievers perceive their work. The far greater challenge is communicating Christianity to a culture whose worldview, language, customs, art, and social structure have been shaped by religious beliefs different from, and often hostile to, biblical Christianity.

Those with little experience of this underestimate the size of the task. One might think it is merely a matter of finding correspondent words, symbols, and media in the target culture, and simply translating from one culture to another. Sometimes that can be done.

But here is the real dilemma: what do you do when the target culture has *no* words for what you need to communicate? What do you do when it has not developed its own writing system to read God's Word? What do you do when its musical instruments have been used mostly for shamanistic ceremonies or for war-dances? What do you do if the commonly practiced form of marriage is unbiblical? What do you do if the form of dress is shameful to the human made in God's image?

According to some contemporary theories, you are not to judge such things. You are there to simply give out the propositional truths of the Gospel. Indeed, some missionaries have been taught the "cellophane-wrapping" view of culture. Culture is nothing more than the wrapping or packaging around the Gospel—meaningless and amoral in itself, simply an instance of varying human preference. Give out the message and leave the cultural customs alone.

Serious missionaries know better. They know that within every culture there will be instances of God's common grace—customs that produced social order, delicious meals, folk tales with moral power, social differentiation, special ceremonies, poems, songs, crafts, and artwork that can be used to illustrate and communicate biblical truths as Paul did with the Greeks when quoting Epimenides, Aratus and Menander.

But they also know that cultures shaped by idolatry will have artwork that communicate idolatry, social customs that reinforce idolatry, and language reflective of idolatry. There will be gaping holes in the vocabulary, musical literacy, and understanding of the world that need to be filled with Christian truth. There will be existing devices, technologies, and customs that cannot be used by Christians without severe confusion or strain on the conscience, which will need to be eliminated altogether or transformed until they are no longer recognizable. Here the missionary is not simply co-opting and adapting what he finds; he is actively adding and removing in the name of helping an infant church learn to walk.

The ability to do this skillfully requires the missionary become expert in two sets of meaning: biblical meaning and cultural meaning. He must know what Christian truth and affection is, which means he cannot be a novice in the faith. He must then learn the meaning of his host culture as completely as time allows. He need not become expert in evil (Romans 16:19), but he should be familiar enough with the culture to be able to readily understand the meaning of a certain musical instrument in the target culture and whether it is consonant with Christian affections. He must continually be comparing Christian meaning with the symbols, devices, tools, customs, technologies, artwork, and media in the target culture. If he is not competent in both systems of meaning, two errors will result.

One, he may ignore the system of meaning present in the culture and simply impose the forms of meaning from his home culture. As we said, the missionary needs to do this where the target culture simply lacks the forms or devices to carry the weight of Christian truth. But the error here is not introducing what is needed, it is ignoring what is present and may helpfully communicate truth. Christianity takes on a more foreign feel than necessary, often becoming a strange outpost of 1950s Americana on another continent. Believe it or not, this is the less serious error.

Two, and more dangerously, he may uncritically adopt the system of meaning in the culture, believing that Christianity will be far more readily received and embraced if clothed in familiar symbols. His error is not simply that he translates the truth, it is that he does not carefully discern if some cultural forms will distort the message of Christianity once adopted. He avoids the ditch of paternalism and swerves over into syncretism.

Missionaries need to be well-versed in the meaning of two worlds and know how to use, adopt, reject, and adapt forms in the target culture so that Christianity may progressively transform a people from "the empty tradition (*anastrophe*) received from [their] fathers" (1 Peter 1:18) into a people with honorable conduct (*anastrophe*) before the world (1 Peter 2:12). He is, whether he means to be or not, a culture-maker and shaper. And who is sufficient for such things?

PAGAN CULTURE AND APOSTATE CULTURE

In discussions of evangelizing the post-modern West, something is often forgotten. Those cultures which were formed by Christianity and have since abandoned it are not reverting to paganism. They are not pagan cultures.

CULTURE

They are apostate cultures, and an apostate culture is a much scarier animal than a pagan one.

C. S. Lewis wrote on how much easier it would be to witness to a pagan culture.

> Christians and Pagans had much more in common with each other than either has with a post-Christian. The gap between those who worship different gods is not so wide as that between those who worship and those who do not....
>
> It is hard to have patience with those Jeremiahs, in Press or pulpit, who warn us that we are "relapsing into Paganism." It might be rather fun if we were. It would be pleasant to see some future Prime Minister trying to kill a large and lively milk-white bull in Westminster Hall. But we shan't. What lurks behind such idle prophecies, if they are anything but careless language, is the false idea that the historical process allows mere reversal; that Europe can come out of Christianity "by the same door as in she went" and find herself back where she was. It is not what happens. A post-Christian man is not a Pagan; you might as well think that a married woman recovers her virginity by divorce. The post-Christian is cut off from

the Christian past and therefore doubly from the Pagan past.[1]

An apostate is treated very differently in Scripture to an infidel. An infidel suppresses the truth of general revelation but has not claimed membership with the people of God. His unbelief is to be rebuked, but he is to be patiently evangelized.

Conversely, an apostate claims to be one of the people of God while denying and opposing the fundamentals of the faith. Entire New Testament books, such as Jude, 2 John, and 2 Peter, give the bulk of their content to identifying and responding to apostates.

What then does apostasy look like on a cultural level? An apostate culture claims to be all the things Christianity brought: virtuous, tolerant of other views, loving, respectful of human freedom, interested in human dignity, peace-loving, concerned with mercy and justice, governed by sound reason, gentle to all, etc. At the same time, it now vociferously renounces the fundamentals of the faith that gave it those things: the inspiration and authority of Scripture, the deity and humanity of Christ, the depravity of man and the need for atonement, the essentiality of faith in grace. It does not want the moniker

---

[1] *De Descriptione Temporum*, Inaugural Lecture from The Chair of Mediaeval and Renaissance Literature at Cambridge University, 1954.

CULTURE

Christian, but it wants the equivalent of the title *righteous*: good person, tolerant, and loving. It wishes to receive all the benefits and privileges that Christianity brought, but it would disown all the responsibilities that Christianity demands: belief, submission, and love of Christ.

We should note that this phenomenon is new, as far as Christianity goes. Israel committed apostasy, too, and the books of the prophets detail what a perverted and warped effect it had on post-Solomonic Israel. But since Christianity was never rooted in one land, it took many years before one could say that Christianity had permeated a culture. And only after the Enlightenment (a misnomer, if there ever was one), do we now encounter a culture apostate from Christianity.

We are only beginning to see the terrifying effects of this. Morality without religion soon becomes a terrifying tyranny. Freedom without grace-enabled submission soon becomes the mere power to assert one's will. Love without a holy God becomes lust in hitherto-unseen forms. Reason unhinged from Revelation and ordinate affection becomes a perverse Pied Piper, leading souls to absurd, and yet "logical," places. Tolerance without worship becomes coercion. When the Christian God is denied, the image of God in man must steadily be abolished, and the result is a nightmarish culture.

Most frightening of all, unlike evangelizing a pagan culture, this culture has heard the Good News. They are not in darkness, needing the light of the gospel to free them from the chains of idolatry. They have seen the light, turned from it, and are not interested in seeing it again. Denials of Christianity's claims are taught in the classroom, the lecture hall, the TV documentary, and often funded with tax-payer money. Our kings and princes know the culture is apostate and would have it so.

How do we evangelize an apostate culture? I'm yet to see the evangelism and missions books take this seriously. What does, "And on some have compassion, making a distinction but others save with fear, pulling *them* out of the fire, hating even the garment defiled by the flesh (Jude 1:22-23)," mean on a cultural level? Should we seek to "redeem" or "transform" the cultural equivalent of a Jehovah's Witness Kingdom Hall?

Perhaps we had best begin weighing up what Scripture says about those who have been enlightened but have fallen. It might influence what we do and don't do to win the lost. It might change whether we think it appropriate to make the lost feel at home in our worship. It might change how we do apologetics as a whole.

MONOCULTURAL UNIFORMITY

Of the little pilot-fish words that swim alongside the more commonly mangled word, *culture*, two of the more frequently heard are *multicultural* and *diversity*. In fact, these have become unquestioned, and probably, unassailable holy words in modern culture. A for-profit company will have somewhere on its Vision and Mission statement, "Our core-values include a commitment to diversity."

Like all mangled words, these represent a vague idea associated with an undefined good. To some, they mean, "to not unfairly privilege one ethnic group over another." To others, they mean something like, "to populate with representatives of many religions, ethnicities, genders, and sexual orientations." While everyone will agree that in a meritocracy, no one should be dismissed or favored because of a genuinely in-born trait (such as skin-color or gender), this is not what *multiculturalism* and *diversity* really have come to mean.

They have really come to mean that the one truth everyone must accept is that there are many truths. What everyone in secularism must bow before is the idea that no culture can be judged better than another, no religion may claim to be truer than another, no gender may be regarded as unequal in strengths and gifts to another (or even forced on one), and no sexual orientation can be claimed as normative or deviant. A commitment to multiculturalism and diversity is a commitment to religious pluralism and moral relativism.

But as is becoming clear, multiculturalism is pluralistic only with those submissive to pluralism. Those who continue to claim their religion is exclusively true, or that

LGBTQ+ sexual orientations are deviant, or that males and females are just that, will soon find an aggressive response more intolerant than the most narrowly rigid ideologies. They will be excoriated in the news media, roundly abused on social media, and perhaps punished legally. It turns out that multiculturalism and diversity are quite committed to a monocultural uniformity to their view of multiculturalism and diversity. Disagree and be punished.

Furthermore, it is not enough to quietly disagree. Multicultural diversity requires you make public acts of penance for ever having held another view. These will include removing or replacing whatever sign, statement, term, practice, or object that in any way insinuates present or historical non-conformity to multicultural diversity. They will include making amends for previous non-conformity by hiring employees that reflect multicultural diversity, by marketing and advertising in ways that reflect multicultural diversity, and by having public relations watchdogs ready to issue apologies and offer reparations for any infringement of multicultural diversity. If they hadn't told us of their enlightened motives, we might even think that multicultural diversity is an oppressive, tyrannical ideology. But as they remind us, it is their opponents who are Nazis. Phew.

CULTURE

Strangely enough, the Bible describes an altogether different kind of diversity. Revelation 7 describes a scene in heaven:

> After these things I looked, and behold, a great multitude which no one could number, of all nations, tribes, peoples, and tongues, standing before the throne and before the Lamb, clothed with white robes, with palm branches in their hands, and crying out with a loud voice, saying, "Salvation belongs to our God who sits on the throne, and to the Lamb!" (Rev. 7:9-10)

Amazingly, this multitude made up of representatives from every historic *ethnos*, tribe, people group and language group, *say the same thing*. This group, diverse in their ethnic origins, are united by their belief in Jesus Christ, praise for His name, and submission to Him. Here is one culture, composed of many ethnicities. Here is one religion, composed of many nations and men and women. Here is one Bride, composed of many tribes, given to one Bridegroom. It is taken for granted that with such a group, they were saved *out* of their religions, *out* of their deviant sexual behavior, and *out* of their false views. This is a uniculture, or monoculture, with complete uniformity in loves and beliefs, composed of the greatest diversity of people groups that will ever be gathered.

The best part is that this diverse monoculture was achieved through persuasion, not coercion. No one has to become a Christian. In obedience to Christ, we do not persecute those who disagree with us, or punish them legally (John 18:36). It was Christianity, and Baptists in particular, that taught the world that the church cannot be a state church, nor should the state enforce religion. The very idea of allowing free men and women to worship according to conscience is a Christian idea, not the brainchild of secular atheists.

The weird paradox is then this: in pursuit of "multicultural diversity" secularists are actually tyrannically enforcing a *de facto* unicultural uniformity. And Christians, in pursuit of a monocultural uniformity (in Heaven) are tolerant of a multicultural, diverse, secular order.

Christians should be committed to fulfilling the Great Commission, which will create the scene in Revelation 7. Christians should be against partiality of all forms: racism, prejudice, and chauvinism. But Christians should not burn incense to the Caesar of multiculturalism and diversity, as the world means those words. To do so will be to deny that Jesus is Lord.

4

EMOTION

Perhaps few words are as mangled as the word *emotion*. This word produces a cacophony of confusion. For some, emotion is nothing more than the superficial states of the body: neither moral, nor important. For others, emotion is the gold standard of sincerity: if you feel it, then you mean it, and lack of feeling is a lack of sincerity. For some, feelings never lie; for others, they nearly always do.

Misunderstanding this word can have catastrophic effects. The ideas associated with emotion lie at the very heart of worship. They enter our understanding of counseling, discipleship, and biblical change. Misunderstanding this word leads to the extremes of stoicism and hedonism, to brutality and sentimentality, to abuse of the body and idolatry of the body. It can lead us to place the emphasis on the mind instead of the heart, or it can lead us to being controlled by bodily appetites instead of the soul's reason.

As with the other words we have studied, much of the problem is equivocation. Emotion means different things in different contexts, and the same person may mean different things by the use of the term, even in the same sentence. In fact, I would say that this particular word has been saddled with the burden of about three or four other ideas.

One of them is motive. What moves or inclines people to action or thought is sometimes called emotion or feeling. "He just doesn't feel very interested in the topic." "She has mixed feelings about speaking in front of those people." "He feels strongly about this cause." Here, emotion or feeling describes how strongly, weakly, or ambiguously someone is inclined to an action. Here, emotion is, in truth, referring to what someone loves or hates.

A second idea which emotion substitutes for is responses of desire or dislike in many forms. The various species of desire are often called emotions: joy, anger, sorrow, fear, disgust, or surprise. Of course, each of these may come in further species. Anger could be fury, irritation, rage, frustration, or bitterness. Joy could be contentment, hilarity, happiness, satisfaction, amusement, pleasure, and so on. Each of these is not simply a difference in degree, but a difference in kind, in actual form. Anger comes in different forms, as does fear, sorrow and surprise. These may be more or less rational, more or less voluntary, or more or less pleasing to God. If you consider the lists of virtues and the lists of sins that the New Testament gives us, you will find on those lists several words which would be named "emotions" by moderns (Mark 7:21-22; Romans 1:29-31; 1 Corinthians 6:9-10; 2

Corinthians 12:20; Galatians 5:19-24; Ephesians 5:3-6; Philippians 4:8; 2 Timothy 3:2-5; James 3:14-17; 2 Peter 1:5-7).

A third idea that moderns mean by emotion is mood or temperament. One's mood can refer to a bodily state of lethargy or excitement, fatigued lowness or anxious alertness, giddy expectation, or cold-sweat dread. General temperament is a strange mix of inherited traits, bodily constitution, unique personality, and learned character habits. As embodied souls, or ensouled bodies, we are beings whose spiritual desires have bodily effects and manifestations, and whose bodies produce effects upon our souls.

Untangling this word will mean separating out these meanings and suggesting some synonyms.

A SHORT HISTORY OF "EMOTION"

Some might be surprised to learn that the word *emotion* is perhaps only 200 years old. Thomas Dixon has documented the history of the term "emotion" in his book *From Passions to Emotions*. He shows that what was originally a moral category in Christian thought—named *affections* or *passions*—became a psychological category termed *emotions*. What used to refer to the inclination of the will or the presence of appetites became subsumed into an idea of passive bodily or neurological responses.

Of course, people have been discussing this topic for centuries, even though the term *emotion* is a newcomer. In the Christian tradition, writers distinguished between the higher, volitional part of the soul that expressed love in the form of affections, and the lower part of the soul (the involuntary or irrational part) which did so in the form of appetitive passions. For Christians, affections were movements of the will in the direction of desire, not whimsical and involuntary bodily experiences.

One sees this thinking very early. For example, Augustine united desire (*cupiditas*), fear (*timor*), joy (*laetitia*), and sorrow (*tristitia*) under the single principle of love (*amor*). Augustine clarifies that the important matter in judging the morality of an "emotion" is its chosen and willed object. "In our ethics, we do not so much inquire whether a pious soul is angry, as *why* he is angry; not whether he is sad, but *what is the cause* of his sadness; not whether he fears, but *what* he fears"[1]. In other words, the object of desire determines the moral quality of the love. Love, according to Augustine, is a matter of inclination towards desired objects. Love is a moral response of positive inclination towards an object. Therefore, the kind of love may vary significantly when the objects desired vary significantly. Put simply, love *corresponds* to its object.

---

[1] City of God, IX, v.

Thomas Aquinas similarly saw love as the direction or inclination of the will towards an object, not as an irrational psychological feeling. In fact, Aquinas saw all "emotions" as love of some form: "Hence love is naturally the first act of the will and appetite; for which reason all the other appetite movements presuppose love, as their root and origin. For nobody desires anything nor rejoices in anything, except as a good that is loved: nor is anything an object of hate except as opposed to the object of love".[2]

For Jonathan Edwards, "affections" were movements of the will informed by the understanding, while passions were more related to appetite:

> The affections and passions are frequently spoken of as the same; and yet in the more common use of speech, there is in some respect a difference; and affection is a word that in its ordinary signification, seems to be something more extensive than passion, being used for all vigorous lively actings of the will or inclination; but passion for those that are more sudden, and whose effects on the animal spirits are more violent, and the mind more overpowered, and less in its own command.[3]

---

[2] *Summa Theologica*, I, xx, Art. I.

[3] Jonathan Edwards, *Religious Affections*, ed. Paul Ramsey, vol. 2, Works of Jonathan Edwards Online (New Haven: Yale University Press, 1754), 98.

In the premodern Christian tradition, love as an affection could, therefore, be appropriate or inappropriate since love could be rightly or wrongly directed. The object of desire determined if it was right to desire such a thing and necessarily dictated the moral quality of the affection.

This changed in the 1700s. In eighteenth-century Germany, a third faculty of the soul, in addition to understanding and will, was introduced—that of *feeling*. This was endorsed in works by Kant and Schopenhauer, who promoted the idea of irrational and involuntary feelings. British moralists of the same period began departing from a will-centered affective psychology and tacitly introduced a three-faculty psychology (understanding, will, and feelings), rather than a two-faculty one (understanding and will).

Thomas Brown (1778–1820) coined the term *emotion* in his 1820 *Lectures on the Philosophy of the Human Mind*. For Brown, only intellectual states were active, while emotions were mere feelings that were passively experienced. This concept would then be co-opted by influential writers such as Thomas Chalmers and, later, by materialists such as Charles Darwin, Herbert Spencer, and Alexander Bain, culminating in its use by William James in 1884, which corresponds somewhat to its use today.

Contemporary evangelicals tend to conflate the concepts of affection and emotion. To do so is very dangerous for at least three reasons. First, such a move conflates moral actions for which we are responsible with bodily appetites over which we often have little control. Second, it elevates what should be largely ignored (bodily moods) and ignores what should be controlled (affective responses). Third, it becomes dismissive toward the quality of our moral affections and what shapes them. These dangers are each worth investigating.

DOES GOD HAVE EMOTIONS?

Trying to answer a badly worded question often leads to an inferior answer. Loaded questions implicate those who even attempt to answer them. "By what authority doest thou these things?" Whether Jesus had answered, "By My own," or, "By My Father's," he would have been accused of pride or blasphemy. Best rule of thumb: ask the questioner of a loaded question to re-phrase the question or avoid answering altogether.

Does God have emotions? This question suffers from the equivocal meaning of the word "emotion." It is impossible to answer without sounding like you are equivocating yourself.

Afrikaans has a phrase "Ja-nee," (pronounced *yah nee-ah*) which is loosely translated as "Well, I suppose," or, "Perhaps," or "Depends." Literally translated, it is exactly "Yes-No." That's about how accurately you could answer the question, "Does God have emotions?"

Yes, He does, and no, He does not. This shows how vapid the word *emotion* is. Here are three theologians explaining how God does and does not have what people today call "emotions."

Thomas Aquinas claims that love can be either an act of the "sensitive appetite," which makes it a passion, or an act of the "intellective appetite," which does not. Aquinas suggests love in God is the latter. God rejoices and delights in what pleases him without desiring out of a sense of need. This distinction would maintain God as an affective being, not a passionate one.[4] God has affections, but not passions.

Jonathan Edwards shows that there are bodily "passions," but God, angels and spirits in heaven possess affections, as do embodied humans. "Feelings" in the body are unique to man, but are not the same as affections:

> But yet it is not the body, but the mind only, that is the proper seat of the affections. The body of man is no more capable of being really the subject of love or hatred, joy or sorrow, fear or hope, than the body of a tree, or than the same body of man is capable of thinking and understanding. As it is the soul only that has ideas, so it is the soul only that is pleased or displeased with its ideas. As it is the soul only that thinks, so it is the soul only that loves or hates, rejoices or is grieved

---

[4] Thomas Aquinas, *Summa Theologica*, XX, i.

at what it thinks of. Nor are these motions of the animal spirits, and fluids of the body, anything properly belonging to the nature of the affections, though they always accompany them, in the present state; but are only effects or concomitants of the affections that are entirely distinct from the affections themselves, and no way essential to them; so that an unbodied spirit may be as capable of love and hatred, joy or sorrow, hope or fear, or other affections, as one that is united to a body").[5]

Finally, C. S. Lewis demonstrates that God's affections are not weaker or colder than what we think of as emotions, but stronger and clearer:

When we wish to learn of the love and goodness of God by *analogy*—by imagining parallels to them in the realm of human relations—we turn of course to the parables of Christ. But when we try to conceive the reality as it may be in itself, we must beware lest we interpret 'moral attributes' in terms of mere conscientiousness or abstract benevolence. *The mistake is easily made because we (correctly) deny that God has passions; and with us a love that is not passionate means a love that is something less. But the reason why God has no passions is that passions imply passivity and intermission. The*

---

[5] Edwards, *Religious Affections*, 98.

passion of love is something that happens to us, as 'getting wet' happens to a body: and God is exempt from that 'passion' in the same way that water is exempt from 'getting wet'. He cannot be affected with love, because He is love. To imagine that love as something less torrential or less sharp than our own temporary and derivative 'passions' is a most disastrous fantasy.[6]

Here we can see the problem with this mangled word *emotion* and perhaps part of the reason why evangelicalism finds itself embroiled in a debate about the impassibility of God. Words matter. Misleading words mislead.

Does God have emotions? Ja-nee. Does God feel? Ja-nee. Does God have affections? Yes. Does God have passions? No.

STOP FEELING YOUR FEELINGS

Since *emotion* is a mangled and confusing word, we need to separate the different experiences it is used to refer to. As we have seen, older generations used the terms *affections* and *passions* to at least attempt to point out the differences. Some of these emotional experiences are moral desires and should be treated with the same caution and care given to any other moral command. Some of these

---

[6] C. S. Lewis, *Miracles* (London, U.K: HarperCollins Publishers, 1947), 148.

EMOTION

emotional experiences are bodily whims and passing moods and should be paid no more heed than hiccups or an itch. In other words, some are matters of the will to be obeyed while others are matters of the body to be simply endured or ignored.

The great problem in modern evangelicalism is it does precisely the reverse: feelings are sought, cultivated and savored, while moral affections are casually ignored and dismissed as neutral and non-moral. In the name of an authentic and lively faith (reacting against cold and bookish Christianity), some groups grab all feelings, fondle them, and give them scrunchy-faced intensity. In the name of a stable and theologically serious faith (reacting against flaky and mystical Christianity), some groups routinely snub Christian affections or send them packing to the room marked "unimportant matters of preference."

So, we end up with two camps, one in each ditch: the sentimentalists obsessed with feeling their feelings, and the brutalists obsessed with maintaining stoic indifference to most affections. In actual practice, the same Christian veers into either ditch at different times.

C. S. Lewis perhaps remains the very best modern theologian of the affections. He has much to say on real Christian affections, particularly in *The Abolition of Man*. At the same time, Lewis never tires of telling Christians to mostly ignore their feelings.

Consider:

Don't bother much about your feelings. When they are humble, loving, brave, give thanks for them; when they are conceited, selfish, cowardly, ask to have them altered. In neither case are they you, but only a thing that happens to you. What matters is your intentions and your behavior.[7]

Obedience is the key to all doors; feelings come (or don't come) and go as God pleases.[8]

Feelings come and go and when they come a good use can be made of them: they cannot be our regular diet.[9]

For these, perhaps, being nearly all will, come from a deeper level than feeling. In feeling there is so much that is really not ours—so much that comes from weather and health or from the last book read. One thing seems certain. It is no good angling for the rich moments.[10]

---

[7] C. S. Lewis, *Yours, Jack: Spiritual Direction From C. S. Lewis*, ed. Paul F. Ford (New York, NY: HarperCollins Publishers, 2008), 169.

[8] Lewis, *Yours, Jack*, 152

[9] C. S. Lewis, *The World's Last Night and Other Essays*, Kindle (New York, NY: Mariner Books, 1952), 144.

[10] C. S. Lewis, *Letters to Malcolm*, Harcourt (New York, NY: Mariner Books, 1964, 1992), 226.

Nobody can always have devout feelings: and even if we could, feelings are not what God principally cares about. Christian Love, either towards God or towards man, is an affair of the will. If we are trying to do His will we are obeying the commandment, 'Thou shalt love the Lord thy God.' He will give us feelings of love if He pleases. We cannot create them for ourselves, and we must not demand them as a right. But the great thing to remember is that, though our feelings come and go, his love for us does not.[11]

Accept these sensations with thankfulness as birthday cards from God, but remember that they are only greetings, not the real gift.... The real thing is the gift of the Holy Spirit which can't usually be—perhaps not ever—experienced as a sensation or emotion. The sensations are merely the response of your nervous system. Don't depend on them. Otherwise when they go and you are once more emotionally flat (as you certainly will be quite soon), you might think that the real thing had gone too. But it won't. It will be there when you can't feel it. May even be most operative when you can feel it least.[12]

---

[11] C. S. Lewis, *Mere Christianity*, Fiftieth Anniversary Edition (London, U.K: HarperCollins Publishers, 2002), 132.

[12] Lewis, *Yours, Jack*, 179.

How do we reconcile these statements with all Lewis has to say on the importance of affections? After all, he wrote a whole book on different kinds of love, *The Four Loves*.

The answer is that in these quotes and in many other places Lewis is dealing with that aspect of the concept *emotion* that is truly non-moral: our bodily and neurological experiences, our moods, our liveliness, our general state of optimism or despondency, our physical sense of alertness to spiritual realities. As Lewis never tires of pointing out, these come and go. They may be given by God, or they may be withheld by God. They may come from a good lunch or the lack thereof. They cannot be willed, or they lose their very nature as spontaneous accompaniment. They are pleasant or terrible companions, but they are just that: fellow travelers that we must tolerate while we live in a fallen world in fallen bodies.

Feelings is a fairly modern term. Theologians in Jonathan Edwards' time spoke of "animal spirits" and "animal fluids" as part of their philosophy of affections and passions. Ancient Greek theories about "choleric," "sanguine" "phlegmatic" and "melancholic" bodily fluids, or humors, were supposed to account for differing moods and temperaments. Theories about moods and emotions have moved on from supposed bodily humors to theories of serotonin in the brain and, in that sense, people are still accounting for certain aspects of human emotional states in the composition or function of the body itself.

EMOTION

When dealing with these matters, Lewis is exactly right. Bodily fluctuations sometimes work to your advantage and, when they do, give thanks. Sometimes they work against you, and, in those moments, you must ignore them or master them. Certainly we should never make our bodily feelings any test of how sincere we are, how devoted we are, or how authentically we are worshipping. Churches or Christian leaders that encourage a pursuit of what amounts to bodily undulations as a litmus test of faith, joy, or love have effectively imprisoned their people in the cells of their aging and changing bodies. Even worse, when "intense feeling" becomes the measure of spirituality, the opposite always results: people begin manufacturing facades of intense feeling, which must be the ultimate insincerity. Since no one can control feeling, but no one is allowed to admit as much, you end up with a crowd of phonies pretending that they have all inexplicably been visited by overpowering religious feelings (again) in the last week. This is the blind leading the blind into a ditch of despair. No one is feeling their feelings like the leaders claim you must, but no one wants to point out that the Emperor has no clothes. So people pretend to have intense feelings, while feeling guilty for not having them when, in reality, no guilt is necessary for the relative state of your body. The only ones not feeling guilty are the ones who actually are guilty: those novices leading the flock into the idolatry of sentimentalism.

We don't need to feel our feelings. We already do. We are to pursue Christian desires—wholeheartedly. We should seek to be affected by the beauty of truth. More on that in the next section.

I WAS AFFECTED VS. I WAS EMOTIONAL

While C. S. Lewis encourages us to not place too much stock in our *feelings*, he was adamant that the whole point of education was to create right *affections*. Affections are not a matter of bodily sensations, but a matter of judging value and responding appropriately:

> Until quite modern times all teachers and even all men believed the universe to be such that certain emotional reactions on our part could be either congruous or incongruous to it—believed, in fact, that objects did not merely receive, but could *merit*, our approval or disapproval, our reverence or our contempt...St Augustine defines virtue as *ordo amoris*, the ordinate condition of the affections in which every object is accorded that kind of degree of love which is appropriate to it. Aristotle says that the aim of education is to make the pupil like and dislike what he ought.[13]

---

[13] C.S. Lewis, *The Abolition of Man* (San Francisco, CA: HarperSanFrancisco, 2001), 14.

EMOTION

> And because our approvals and disapprovals are thus recognitions of objective value or responses to an objective order, therefore emotional states can be in harmony with reason (when we feel liking for what ought to be approved) or out of harmony with reason (when we perceive that liking is due but cannot feel it). No emotion is, in itself, a judgement; in that sense all emotions and sentiments are alogical. But they can be reasonable or unreasonable as they conform to Reason or fail to conform. The heart never takes the place of the head: but it can, and should, obey it.[14]

In other words, there is something else going on in the human soul that is today termed "emotion." There are the soul's inclinations, approvals, and desires. These are not irrational, inchoate sensations of the brain or body. They are the desires of the heart, informed by the intellect and accompanied, to a greater or lesser degree, by "feelings."

McClymond & McDermott explain the difference in the thinking of Jonathan Edwards:

> [Many], have wrongly assumed that Edwards's affections were the same thing as "emotions." But emotions for Edwards were only one dimension of human experience shaped by affections, along with thinking and

---

[14] Lewis, *Abolition of Man*, 19.

choosing. Edwards argued that true religious affections sometimes choose *against* emotional feeling, such as when Jesus chose not to yield to his feelings of fear in the Garden of Gethsemane. When "passions" overwhelm one's better judgment, as in a fit of rage, emotions are in fact opposed to true religious affections. Furthermore, Edwards always linked affections to an object, while emotions may or may not have an object. In current English usage, the statement "I am emotional" need not imply an object of emotion. But the assertion "I am affectionate" raises the question, "Toward what or whom?"[15]

To put it another way, affections are rational responses to something outside of our own psychology. We could try to find synonyms for *affections* to replace the word *emotions*. We might call them "strongly felt intellectual desires." We might try "the heart's leading inclination," "the soul's treasured pursuit," or the "the mind's deepest love." All of these lack the precision we want and leave something out. But they contain at least the following notions that clear up the fogginess of the word "emotion":

---

[15] Michael J. McClymond and Gerald R. McDermott, *The Theology of Jonathan Edwards*, (New York, NY: Oxford University Press, 2012), Kindle edition, loc 4960.

EMOTION

1. Affections are not irrational sensations; they are the intelligent and chosen acts of the will.

2. Affections are not mere passing preferences or intellectual observations; they move the soul to actions and choice.
3. Affections are not only cold acts of reason; they are acts of love and desire towards an object of beauty. They are judgments of value that move the soul to action.
4. Affections are not a separate faculty of human psychology. They are the strong desires and acts of the human will which already contains intellectual judgment.

In summary, much of the problem is the wrong-headed anthropology of "mind, will and emotions" so popular today in both secular and Christian psychology and counseling. Scripture never upholds this distinction. Instead, it speaks most often of the "heart," which in both Hebrew and New Testament thought was the seat of intellectual judgment and volitional desire.

The immaterial part of man has a unified intellectual and volitional ability. But not all that the mind knows does the will love or choose. When what is known becomes *beautiful* to us, our desires and inclinations pursue it, and affections such as love, joy, hope, fear, and courage accompany the choice. Sometimes we "feel" these affections more sensibly than at other times. This has more to do with the material part of man. When the feelings assist us, we can be thankful, but at times we must choose against them, and continue to pursue our heart's chosen object of beauty.

By contrast, the "emotional" man pursues felt emotional sensation, regardless of the worth of the object, or the reasonableness of the pursuit. He is not concerned with objective value, with truth or with virtue. According to Paul, "his god is his belly" (Philippians 3:19) because he is led and controlled by his bodily appetites for felt sensations. He does not need to be a drunkard or a philanderer to be so. He need only be a glutton for "happy feelings" or an addict of "amusement escape," and he falls into the category of the man controlled by passions and not affections.

EVERYTHING IS UH-SIM

"How're you guys doin' today?"

"Fine, thanks."

"*Uh-sim.* Will you be using a rewards card today?"

"Uh, no."

EMOTION

"*Uh-sim.* Cash back?"

"No, not today." *Swipes card; takes receipt.*

"No prob. You guys have an *uh-sim* day!"

I'm probably not being fair to the cashiers at Target, but that was certainly how their pronunciation of *awesome* sounded to my ears. But it is entirely fair to say that, in their usage, *awesome* could be substituted with the words *nice, great, good,* or even *okay.* There's no small irony that a word that denotes trembling amazement is now a synonym for things easy, familiar, and casual.

Without being overly scrupulous about how people are using words, such usage is surely a sign that the culture no longer pays attention to the concept of awe or reverence. To speak of an awesome hamburger or an awesome hotdog is to either misunderstand hamburgers and hotdogs or to misunderstand awe. Hamburgers and hotdogs evoke pleasure, excitement, laughter, and heartburn, but not awe. In a moment of awe, a human is overwhelmed with something vastly superior to him in beauty, power, and size, something possibly threatening and dangerous to him, something unfamiliar, uncontrollable, and, in some ways, unknowable. Responses of awe include silence, wonder, amazement, fear, humility, gratitude, and submission.

The point is, the pleasure of a hotdog and the pleasure of beholding the galaxies are fundamentally *different pleasures*. They are not the same thing directed at different objects. This is precisely why we mean different things by *horror, terror, despair, dread, timidity, panic, trepidation, intimidation, awe, sobriety,* and *reverence*. We use different words because the objects we encounter are different in nature and call for corresponding responses. These words for different affective responses are not interchangeable.

This is why we can speak of ordinate affection, but not of *ordinate emotion*. The impreciseness of the word *emotion* means that it partly refers to feelings. Feelings, being so much more a matter of the body and the appetites, are irrational. But when the heart understands the true nature of what it is encountering, it can choose to respond truthfully, or rationally. Such a response is our "reasonable service" (Romans 12:2). It can see the glory of God and respond with awe—this would be ordinate affection. It can see the glory of God and respond with irreverent casualness—this would be inordinate affection. Affections can be rightly ordered in the same way that doctrine can be true or false. The rational soul can respond with right desire, right love, or wrong desire and wrong love. Again, how deeply it *feels* these affections is not the important matter. What matters is if the heart is inclined toward an object of value with inclinations that match its value.

EMOTION

If everything is uh-sim, then nothing is awesome. And if nothing is awesome, worship is impossible and meaningless.

AFFECT OR EFFECT?

The difference between affections and emotions is seen in what art is used in worship. Since worship uses art, worship leaders can use it in precisely one of these two ways: to affect us, or to create effect.

They can work with poetry, music, and the spoken word to engage the imagination. There the worshipper can contemplate the invisible God for who He is and be affected by truth. As Edwards pointed out, this "impression" is made during corporate worship:

> The main benefit that is obtained by preaching is by impression made upon the mind in the time of it, and not by an effect that arises afterwards by a remembrance of what was delivered. And though an after remembrance of what was heard in a sermon is oftentimes very profitable; yet, for the most part, that remembrance is from an impression the words made on

the heart in the time of it; and the memory profits as it renews and increases that impression.[16]

Once corporate worship is over, the worshipper is returned to regular life with his desires and inclinations more focused on the kind of God he claims to know and love.

Conversely, worship leaders can also work with poetry, music, and the spoken word to simply achieve effect. They can aim to create an experience in which the worshipper experiences immediately—one might say, *viscerally*—the supposed experience of God. God is not contemplated with the understanding; the appetites and feelings are targeted directly, and the resultant experience is associated with God. The worshipper leaves corporate worship and returns to the rest of his life with the creation of an addiction: he will need more of the same next week to feel anything for God. Ironically, these descendants of the Reformers have created a kind of evangelical Mass: the presence of God is only known and felt at church. This time, the Presence is manifest not when the priest rings the bell, but when Dude strums his Fender Stratocaster.

---

[16] Jonathan Edwards, *Some Thoughts Concerning the Present Revival of Religion in New England*, in Edwards, *The Great Awakening*, ed. C. C. Goen, Vol. 4 of *Works of Jonathan Edwards* (New Haven, CT: Yale University Press, 1972), 397.

EMOTION

There are almost limitless ways of creating an effect: the effect of dreamy intimacy with God achieved by a breathy worship leader narrating a quasi-romantic prayer to Jesus over softly playing chords, the effect of sympathy for the cause of Jesus by impassioned pleas for people to come forward while a sentimental hymn is played in the background, the effect of jubilation achieved by a sweaty worship leader literally jumping to the pulsating physicality of music played at volumes only possible with electronic amplification, and so on. If an *effect* is needed, a *technique* can be engineered. However, there is a simple term for this kind of approach, one that many contemporary worship proponents would bristle at: *manipulation*.

There is nothing accidental here. Worship leaders know what kind of art will produce what kind of result. Philosopher Roger Scruton tells us the difference between real art and manipulative art:

> Genuine art also entertains us; but it does so by creating a distance between us and the scenes that it portrays: a distance sufficient to engender disinterested sympathy for the character, rather than vicarious emotions of our own. [17]

---

[17] Scruton, *Beauty*, 102.

Scruton goes on to argue that true art works with imagination, representing ideas for our contemplation. These help us to pursue realities precisely because there is a distance between us and the things we contemplate. Manipulative art works with fantasy, trying to grip or excite us with a supposed portrayal of reality in which we get surrogate fulfilment of desires. Real art takes us out of reality, teaches us, and returns us changed: our desires are more focused on the worth of objects in reality. False art takes us out of reality, mimics it, and gives us substitute emotional experiences purely for self-gratification. It also returns us to reality different: our emotions dissipated through a substitute reality, and a little more dependent on or expectant of such manipulative techniques to feel anything. One kind of art grows our affections; the other shrivels them.

When Scruton speaks of the distance that true art creates between us and what it portrays, it reminds one of the way the Lord has set up worship in contrast to the orgiastic worship of the pagans. In the Old Testament and the New, God simultaneously respects the rational humanity of man and calls for true worship of Himself grounded in the understanding. He does this by portraying Himself in serious, non-manipulative works of imaginative art: the narratives, psalms, metaphors, prophecies, and commands of Scripture.

EMOTION

When believers have followed God's pattern, they have written songs, poems and prayers that reach the understanding through the imagination, which slowly (painfully slowly, sometimes) move and shape the affections. For the one for whom worship has become an itch that needs to be scratched weekly, God's approach is intolerably slow and dull. Such a man wants a clamorous appeal to his appetites, which respond automatically, sensually, and ephemerally. Esau would like a bowl of soup *now*, please. What good do these hymns, promises and principles do for my bored & achin' heart *right now, man*?

By contrast, the result of a slow and patient appeal to the imaginative understanding of regenerate man is a deeply grounded love for God that is ordinate, not a fleeting response that evaporates once the marionette strings stop tugging.

We're told that the worship wars are over, and it is obvious which side has lost. So be it. As Eliot said, "We fight for lost causes because we know that our defeat and dismay may be the preface to our successors' victory, though that victory itself will be temporary; we fight rather to keep something alive than in the expectation that it will triumph."

VOTES FROM THE DEMOCRACY OF THE DEAD

The idea of ordinate affection is not welcome today. Narcissism has become a celebrated virtue, and is now even given the monikers *transparent*, *authentic*, and *real*. The two ditches of sentimentalism and brutality now take up most of the road and a slender middle path of appropriate love is known by few and trod by fewer. Amusement is now the dominant mode for transmitting and receiving knowledge, so if it doesn't entertain me, it may not be true. A life of vicarious wish-fulfilment in popular movies and music keep us feeling our feelings, while nostalgia and familiarity in pop culture keep us feeling full, even when we have not been fed. A culture of despair and nihilistic boredom is anesthetized through constant diversion.

To speak to this culture of *ordinate* affection, right loves, orthopathy, or appropriate sentiment is to invite everything from indifferent dismissal to scorn to incensed outrage. It is not uncommon to have the discussion of affections labelled "ideological," "elitist," "esoteric," or "speculative," even by professing Christians.

But *he who knows only his own generation remains forever a child*, said Santayana. Ordinate affection is neither a novel nor an abstruse concept. Consider:

EMOTION

Augustine (354–430): When the miser prefers his gold to justice, it is through no fault of the gold, but of the man; and so with every created thing. For though it be good, it may be loved with an evil as well as with a good love: it is loved rightly when it is loved ordinately; evilly, when inordinately... So that it seems to me that it is a brief but true definition of virtue to say, it is the order of love; and on this account, in the Canticles, the bride of Christ, the city of God, sings, "Order love within me."[18]

Now he is a man of just and holy life who forms an unprejudiced estimate of things, and keeps his affections also under strict control, so that he neither loves what he ought not to love, nor fails to love what he ought to love, nor loves that more which ought to be loved less, nor loves that equally which ought to be loved either less or more, nor loves that less or more which ought to be loved equally. No sinner is to be loved as a sinner; and every man is to be loved as a man for God's sake; but God is to be loved for His own sake.[19]

He loves thee too little, who loves anything with thee which he loves not for thy sake.[20]

---

[18] Augustine, *City of God*, XV, xxii.
[19] Augustine, *On Christian Doctrine*, I, xxvii.
[20] Augustine, *Confessions*, IX, xxix.

Bernard of Clairvaux (1090-1153): We are to love God for Himself, because of a twofold reason; nothing is more reasonable, nothing more profitable.[21]

You want me to tell you why God is to be loved and how much. I answer, the reason for loving God is God Himself; and the measure of love due to Him is immeasurable love.[22]

The anonymous author of *Theologia Germanica*, (late 14th century): And where a creature loveth other creatures for the sake of something that they have, or loveth God, for the sake of something of her own, it is all false Love; and this Love belongeth properly to nature, for nature as nature can feel and know no other love than this; for if ye look narrowly into it, nature as nature loveth nothing beside herself. But true Love is taught and guided by the true Light and Reason, and this true, eternal and divine Light teacheth Love to love nothing but the One true and Perfect Good, and that simply for its own sake, and not for the sake of a reward, or in the hope of obtaining anything, but

---

[21] Bernard of Clairvaux, *On Loving God*, I.
[22] Bernard of Clairvaux, *On Loving God.*, I.

simply for the Love of Goodness, because it is good and hath a right to be loved."[23]

Thomas Traherne (1636-1674): Can you accomplish the end for which you were created, unless you be Righteous? Can you then be Righteous, unless you be just in rendering to Things their due esteem? All things were made to be yours; and you were made to prize them according to their value: which is your office and duty, the end for which you were created, and the means whereby you enjoy....For then we please God when we are most like Him. We are like Him when our minds are in frame. Our minds are in frame when our thoughts are like His. And our thoughts are then like His when we have such conceptions of all objects as God hath, and prize all things according to their value.[24]

François Fénelon (1651-1715): Men have a great repugnance to this truth, and consider it to be a very hard saying, because they are lovers of self from self-interest. They understand, in a general and superficial way, that they must love God more than all his creatures, but they have no conception of loving God more

---

[23] Anonymous, *Theologia Germanica*, XLII.

[24] Thomas Traherne, *Centuries of Meditations*, First Century, XII.

than themselves, and loving themselves only for Him. They can utter these great words without difficulty, because they do not enter into their meaning, but they shudder when it is explained to them, that God and his glory are to be preferred before ourselves and everything else to such a degree that we must love his glory more than our own happiness, and must refer the latter to the former, as a subordinate means to an end.[25]

Henry Scougal (1650-1678): The worth and excellency of a soul is to be measured by the object of its love. [26]

Jonathan Edwards (1703-1758): For if we love him not for his own sake, but for something else, then our love is not terminated on him, but on something else, as its ultimate object. That is no true value for infinite worth, which implies no value for that worthiness in itself considered, but only on the account of something foreign. Our esteem of God is fundamentally defective, if it be not primarily for the excellency of his nature, which is the foundation of all that is valuable in him in any respect. If we love not God because he is

---

[25] Francois Fénelon,, *Spiritual Progress*, III.

[26] Henry Scougal, *The Life of God in the Soul of Man* (Ross-shire, U.K.: Christian Focus Publications Ltd, 1996), 70.

what he is, but only because he is profitable to us, in truth we love him not at all.[27]

C. S. Lewis (1898-1963): The form of the desired is in the desire. It is the object which makes the desire harsh or sweet, coarse or choice, 'high' or 'low.' It is the object that makes the desire itself desirable or hateful.[28]

And to bring it into this century, with no evangelical axe to grind, here is philosopher Roger Scruton:

Roger Scruton (1944-2020): For a free being, there is right feeling, right experience and right enjoyment just as much as right action. The judgement of beauty orders the emotions and desires of those who make it. It may express their leisure and their taste: but it is pleasure in what they value and taste for their true ideals.[29]

---

[27] Jonathan Edwards, *Original Sin*, ed. C. A Holbrook, vol. 3, *Works of Jonathan Edwards*, 144.

[28] C. S. Lewis, *Surprised by Joy* (New York, NY: Houghton Mifflin Harcourt., 2012), 256.

[29] Scruton, *Beauty*, 197.

5

EQUALITY

Equality is one of those ideas whose basic meaning is understood, but whose presence is demanded where it cannot possibly be expected. After all, equality is a fairly simple concept: when two amounts are equal, neither is greater or lesser than the other. But while equality in mathematics is a simple matter, equality in human affairs is vastly more complex.

Understanding the difference between equal opportunity and equal ability is what gets lost in modern discussions. Equal treatment does not mean equal outcomes.

When two people are equal before the law, neither has an advantage or disadvantage in the court before the case has been heard. That does not mean both are equally innocent, equally guilty, or will receive equally capable legal representation. It just means neither is prejudiced by the court because of ethnicity, sex, or economic state.

When it is said that men and women are equal, those words can be taken as a loose generalization of the statement that husbands and wives are "co-heirs of the grace of life." Both equally receive salvation, the promises of God, and His enablement for life. It does not mean that both are equally capable of defending the home or nurturing infants. It does not mean that the roles in the house must be exactly shared in equal halves. It does not mean that husbands and wives should do exactly what the other one does.

Unfortunately, equality has come to mean something very different from equality before the law, or equality of worth before God. It has come to mean that social planners must eliminate God-given differences, manipulate providential circumstances, and meticulously tinker with the scale of fairness until they are sure that their idea of equality has been achieved.

Their idea of equality might be imagined thus. Imagine some top sprinters lining up for a race. Previously, equality meant that all start behind the same line, all begin at exactly the same moment, and all run exactly 100 meters. In its mangled form, equality would mean determining if one of the sprinters were previously advantaged by being wealthy enough to afford good training and, if so, putting his starting blocks back by a meter or so. If it turns out that another sprinter experienced poverty at some point in his life with a corresponding period of malnutrition, his starting blocks should be put ahead by a few meters. We then find out that one of the sprinters is unusually tall and powerful, and this seems to confer an unfair genetic advantage, so he is forced to run without shoes. One turns out to have had almost no coaching at all, so he is positioned a quarter of the way up the track. When another is discovered to be the grandson of a famous sprinter and the recipient of inherited wealth, his starting blocks are removed, and he is given earmuffs to slow his reaction to the gun. The starting line-up seems over-represented with people of African descent, and a truly representative running race should have some Asians and Caucasians. Four faster African athletes are removed and replaced with four slower Asian and Caucasian sprinters.

When we now look at this ridiculous result, what do we see? An eclectic mix of men spread all over the track in all kinds of states and not even the fastest men on earth. The very last thing we would now conclude is that matters are now *equal* and that now the race will be "a fair fight." But our social planners would ignore the evidence of their eyes and happily conclude that they have now "leveled the playing field," "redressed the inequalities of the past," and "assisted the previously disadvantaged." Instead, all they have done is create a ludicrous situation that no longer even resembles a race. They have confused equality with Cosmic Justice, and the result is not equality. In fact, they have removed the very thing that makes a race interesting: how the abilities of one will triumph over the others if all run an equal distance at the same moment. It is as if the social planners actually wish life to always result in a tie in which there are no winners or losers.

The problem with pursuing Cosmic Justice is its refusal to accept that some inequalities are not morally necessary to correct. Some are quite tolerable. Some actually stimulate great feats of competitive effort. Some are in the nature of things. Some are brought about by history and providence. Some have been developed through hard work. Some exist because of laziness and self-destructive behavior. Some appear accidental. Some are unfortunate results of living in a fallen world. Inequality has innumerable reasons for its presence, and only someone with omniscience and omnipotence would be able to know when, why and how to perfectly "re-balance the scales." In fact, Christians believe He does and will.

But attempting to tinker with life to bring about Cosmic Justice in this way reveals a massive misunderstanding of what equality is and what kind of equality can be, or should be, reasonably pursued.

EQUALITY AND DISTINCTIONS

Those who believe in cosmic justice are actually at war with nature. If you desire that all people have absolutely equal opportunities (as in our sprint race example) by manipulating all kinds of variables, you are actually fighting against the created order. You are fighting biology, genetics, and, indeed, providence.

If you are a cosmic justice devotee, you resent the idea that those who are biologically male should be placed in roles where they seem better suited than those who are biologically female. Indeed, you will wage war over those words "better suited," enlisting examples of female soldiers, female bodyguards, female oil-rig welders, and so on, showing that any distinction is purely a social construct, or even an arbitrary prejudice.

For that matter, someone like this may be at war with other variables of the created order: someone's native intelligence, talents, interests, and dispositions. All that seems determined by forces outside the cosmic justice devotee's worldview must be challenged.

Tragically, some Christians begin breathing in this air and exhaling it with a Christian twist. For example, a favorite hijacked text is Galatians 3:28:

> There is neither Jew nor Greek, there is neither slave nor free, there is neither male nor female; for you are all one in Christ Jesus.

"There!" says the cosmic justice-monger, "doesn't that just prove that the gospel is all about removing distinctions and inequalities?" Well, in a word, *no*. The gospel eliminates any grounds for boasting a human might use to claim special favor with God: sex, class, ethnicity, or some other trait or qualification. In Christ, these distinctions give no one an advantage or disadvantage. In Christ, none of these hinder table fellowship and spiritual equality. But that is a far cry from the removal of distinctions.

Far from it. Paul gives different roles to men and women in corporate worship (1 Timothy 2:8-15) and even for informal church life (Titus 2:1-8). He acknowledges that the class system of Roman life is the order of the day and calls for Christian masters and slaves to behave in exemplary ways (Ephesians 6:5-9). For that matter, in Romans 14, Paul is probably referencing how Jewish Christians may behave differently from Gentile Christians in respect to diet and the observance of days, and he does not call for these differences to stop but to be tolerated and respected with deference and considerateness. From Paul's perspective, differences in ethnicity, class, or gender are part of life and the Christian is not called to erase or resist them.

But what of those inequalities brought about not by biology or genetics, but by injustice—either the injustice of human society, or the apparent injustice of the universe? What of people born to an ethnic group that is enslaved, despised, or mistreated? Or people born in poor circumstances, with little chance to improve? Or people born into a system that targets them for oppression? Should we not wage war on the injustice that gave them a disadvantage?

Perhaps, if rightly defined. Christians wage war by casting down systems of thought that oppose God (2 Corinthians 10:5-6). Christianity's view of man ultimately fermented Rome's cultural life to where it could no longer function as it once had. Christianity's view of man brought about the Magna Carta, balancing the divine right of kings with the *imago dei*. In some cases, Christians have worked actively in politics. In most cases, Christians have been faithful Christians in their vocations and allowed their view to salt the culture.

Christians can also work to faithfully reverse or counter the effects of the curse, whether it is dealing with disease, catastrophe, or some area of the natural order that harms or threatens life. Christians may not understand God's providence in giving some less, or the place of deformity or disease, but they can seek to heal and assist.

Christians do not fight injustice by artificially privileging victims or descendants of injustice over others. Christians do not fight injustice by pretending that the vision of a blind man is adequate, or that the illiterate can read, or that the unlearned can lead. Christians do not fight injustice when they place their finger on the scale, trying to act on a level that belongs to God. We cannot fight the truth of injustice with the fictions of our own benevolent intentions.

We cannot wage war on the past. We cannot re-direct the river of history. We can only help hard-working people in the present and have mercy on those harmed or destitute by something other than their own laziness. Societies that allow hard-working people to succeed are just. Ancient Israel was more than just, it was also merciful:

providing means for the poor to survive (Leviticus 19:10). But notice, the poor still had to work and glean the corners of the vineyard.

Ancient Israel did not fight against the very concept of the poor. It accepted that such would always be the case in a fallen world, and they made merciful provisions for those who would work with the strength they had. They were interested in merciful justice, not cosmic justice. They were concerned with an equal right to survive, not an equal experience of life.

EQUALITY IS MEDICINE, NOT FOOD

I do not think that equality is one of those things (like wisdom or happiness) which are good simply in themselves and for their own sakes. I think it is in the same class as medicine, which is good because we are ill, or clothes which are good because we are no longer innocent. I don't think the old authority in kings, priests, husbands, or fathers, and the old obedience in subjects, laymen, wives, and sons, was in itself a degrading or evil thing at all. I think it was intrinsically as good and beautiful as the nakedness of Adam and Eve. It was rightly taken away because men became bad and abused it. To attempt to restore it now would be the same error as that of the

Nudists. Legal and economic equality are absolutely necessary remedies for the Fall, and protection against cruelty.

> But medicine is not good. There is no spiritual sustenance in flat equality. It is a dim recognition of this fact which makes much of our political propaganda sound so thin. We are trying to be enraptured by something which is merely the negative condition of the good life. That is why the imagination of people is so easily captured by appeals to the craving for inequality, whether in a romantic form of films about loyal courtiers or in the brutal form of Nazi ideology. The tempter always works on some real weakness in our own system of values—offers food to some need which we have starved.[1]

According to Lewis, legal and economic equality is a convention we use to protect ourselves from one another. In other words, centuries of human abuse have revealed that while inequalities most certainly exist, we are seldom prepared to deal rightly with these inequalities when we're in a position to exploit them. Those physically weaker, financially poorer, or even intellectually less capable are almost always exploited by their superiors. It

---

[1] *"Equality," in* C. S. Lewis, *Compelling Reason*, ed. Walter Hooper (London, U.K: William Collins, 1996), 27.

was the biblical religion that first rebuked this tendency, calling on Israel to care for the three groups most easily exploited: orphans, widows, and the poor.

Centuries of jurisprudence and political thought were necessary for the implications of these ideas to germinate and reach full bud: that every human being was to receive exactly equal treatment before the law, and that every person was to be part of a collective decision-making process that would protect us from the abuse of power by one or a few. Legal and political equality became one of the checks and balances of a free society.

Conversely, Lewis believes our intrinsic inequality is actually a splendid and beautiful variety. "In the same way, under the necessary outer covering of legal equality, the whole hierarchical dance and harmony of our deep and joyously accepted spiritual inequalities should be alive." Created differences, differences in appearance, ability, intelligence, talents, or gifts are not a thing to be despised, but celebrated. And we celebrate them when we respect hierarchy, orders, and roles in society, the family, and the church.

This freedom is now devolving into tyranny, as those obsessed with equality now pursue it for opposite reasons from the Christian thinkers of the past. In their thinking, it is not man's evil and propensity to harm others that requires legal equality; it is actually man's innate goodness and propensity to excel that requires actual, enforced equality of outcomes. Inequality represents cosmic injustice and requires correction. We must no longer simply say that men and women are equal before the law; we must ensure that we have an exactly equal number of female plumbers and male kindergarten teachers. We must no longer say that two citizens have an equal right to participate in government, we must insist that those two citizens receive the same schooling and have exactly the same grades.

This is a deep disease of the soul which slowly kills a society. Lewis, again:

> When equality is treated not as a medicine or a safety-gadget, but as an ideal, we begin to breed that stunted and envious sort of mind which hates all superiority. That mind is the special disease of democracy, as cruelty and servility are the special diseases of privileged societies. It will kill us all if it grows unchecked. The man who cannot conceive a joyful and loyal obedience on the one hand, nor an unembarrassed and noble acceptance of that obedience on the other—the man who has never even wanted to kneel or to bow—is a prosaic barbarian.[2]

The reason that the idol of Equality will kill its followers is that they will tyrannically enforce it on the world while

---

[2] Lewis, *Compelling Reason*, 28.

gorging themselves on perverted inequality elsewhere. "Where men are forbidden to honor a king they honor millionaires, athletes, or film-stars instead—even famous prostitutes or gangsters. For spiritual nature, like bodily nature, will be served—deny it food and it will gobble poison."

Behold the society in which you live: where porn stars (famous prostitutes) are celebrated, while recognizing distinctions between men and women can be a criminal offence.

EQUALITY AND NECESSARY HIERARCHY

The current proponents of social justice have little idea of what they may be creating in pursuit of their goal. Their goal is a just society, but the pursuit of radical egalitarianism won't provide them with that.

Richard Weaver, writing in 1948, describes how radical egalitarianism provides nothing new that traditional societies didn't already produce, and may actually be producing a cancerous envy that will destroy society from within. It promises a fiction, and the frustration from pursuing a non-existent and impossible order creates growing angst and unhappiness.

> Equality is a disorganizing concept in so far as human relationships mean order. It is order without a design;

EQUALITY

it attempts a meaningless and profitless regimentation of what has been ordered from time immemorial by the scheme of things. No society can rightly offer less than equality before the law; but there can be no equality of condition between youth and age or between the sexes; there cannot be equality even between friends. The rule is that each shall act where he is strong; the assignment of identical roles produces first confusion and then alienation, as we have increasing opportunity to observe. Not only is this disorganizing heresy busily confounding the most natural social groupings, it is also creating a reservoir of poisonous envy. How much of the frustration of the modern world proceeds from starting with the assumption that all are equal, finding that this cannot be so, and then having to realize that one can no longer fall back on the bond of fraternity!

However paradoxical it may seem, fraternity has existed in the most hierarchical organizations; it exists, as we have just noted, in that archetype of hierarchy, the family. The essence of co-operation is *congeniality*, the feeling of having been "born together." Fraternity directs attention to others, equality to self; and the passion for equality is simultaneous with the growth of egotism. The frame of duty which fraternity erects is itself the source of ideal conduct. Where men feel that society means station, the highest and the lowest see their endeavors contributing to a common end, and they are in harmony rather than in competition. It will be found as a general rule that those parts of the world which have talked least of equality have in the solid fact of their social life exhibited the greatest fraternity. Such was true of feudal Europe before people succumbed to various forms of the proposal that every man should be king. Nothing is more manifest than that as this social distance has diminished and all groups have moved nearer equality, suspicion and hostility have increased. In the present world there is little of trust and less of loyalty. People do not know what to expect of one another. Leaders will not lead, and servants will not serve.

It is a matter of common observation, too, that people meet most easily when they know their position. If their work and authority are defined, they can proceed on fixed assumptions and conduct themselves without embarrassment toward inferior and superior. When the rule of equality obtains, however, no one knows where he belongs. Because he has been assured that he is "just as good as anybody else," he is likely to suspect that he is getting less than his deserts, Shakespeare concluded his wonderful discourse on degree with reference to "an envious fever." And when Mark Twain, in the role of Connecticut Yankee, undertook to destroy the hierarchy of Camelot, he was

EQUALITY

furious to find that serfs and others of the lower order were not resentful of their condition. He adopted then the typical Jacobin procedure of instilling hatred of all superiority. Resentment, as Richard Hertz has made plain, may well prove the dynamite which will finally wreck Western society....

It is generally assumed that the erasing of all distinctions will usher in the reign of pure democracy. But the inability of pure democracy to stand for something intelligible leaves it merely a verbal deception. If it promises equality before the law, it does no more than empires and monarchies have done and cannot use this as a ground to assert superiority. If it promises equality of condition, it promises injustice, because one law for the ox and the lion is tyranny."[3]

A THEOLOGY OF EQUALITY

When God made humankind, He made them male and female, both equally in His image (Genesis 1:26-27). According to Peter, this makes men and women co-heirs of the grace of life (1 Peter 3:7). He chose to do so in a staggered fashion, however, creating the male first, followed by the female. In so doing, God created and exemplified an order: the man would be the spiritual leader (1 Timothy 2:12-13).

---

[3] Weaver, *Ideas Have Consequences*, 42-44.

The Fall introduced depravity into the male-female relationship (Genesis 3:16), men dominating women through sheer strength, and women desiring to usurp men's role of leadership. In Christ, the abuses and enmity between the sexes can be erased with both finding their fullest identity in Him (Galatians 3:28). By the grace of Christ, husbands can again be chivalrous, loving leaders, and women can be strong, supportive companions (Ephesians 5:22-33).

All ethnicities are ultimately one race: the human race (Acts 17:26). God allowed and even separated different nations as an act of simultaneous judgment and mercy (Genesis 11:6-9; Acts 17:26-27). The development of these different ethnic groupings both retarded the depravity and rebellion of the human race and allowed the common grace of God to work separately in each (Acts 14:16-17; 17:27). The degree that each ethnicity rebelled against the light given to them explains the relative distance of the resulting cultures from biblical norms and truths. Some were closer in morals and practices to biblical ideals; some were much further away (Romans 1:18-32). Ethnicities that were exposed to the Gospel and responded positively to it had the privilege of shaping their norms and practices around revealed truth.

In Christ, ethnic hatred, pride, and partiality is a thing of the past (Galatians 3:28; Colossians 3:11; James 2:1-10). Though Israel retains its place as a chosen ethnicity for

EQUALITY

God's own purposes (Romans 9:5-6; 11:1-6), believers now partake of a new, shared identity as one new humanity in Christ (Ephesians 2:11-22). Just as male and female differences do not disappear in Christ, nor do ethnic idiosyncrasies and traits, which even Paul noted about the Cretans (Titus 1:12-13). The point is, these will either be transformed by Christ, or become part of the glorious variety that makes up the redeemed (Revelation 5:9). Believers can no longer use ethnic differences as a point of division or separation within the body of Christ.

When God made man, He instructed man to spread His glory throughout the Earth by subjugating it to intelligent and orderly design (Genesis 1:26-28). This would require a vast variety of abilities, gifts, and talents. Even after the Fall, this variety is not lost, with men specializing in agriculture (Genesis 4:20), music (4:21), and metallurgy (4:22). Men chose leaders, kings, and priests as far back as we can tell. Systems of government and societal structure were, once again, as good or as bad as they were close to or distant from God's truth. Brutal and inhumane systems emerge very early.

The stratification of society is not regarded as an evil, however. Israel's law makes room for leaders, elders, judges, priests, and kings. It allows for indentured servanthood to pay off debts. It predicts that poor people will remain a fixture of society and calls for compassion and generosity for those poor willing to work. It predicts that some Israelites will be wealthy and insists that their wealth is not to give them an advantage in the law courts. It does not penalize them for being wealthy, but it prevents their wealth from perverting justice.

In the New Testament, Paul accepts as a reality the fact that the church may be composed of the lower classes (1 Corinthians 1:26-27). He tells the Corinthians that it is God's plan to have a Body composed of members who are very different in function, ability, and presentability (12:11-27). He cautions them against coveting another's position, denigrating their own, or being puffed up about themselves. But he does not call for uniformity in status or position. All are to be cherished and loved, but some are worthy of double honor (1 Timothy 5:17). Some are to be esteemed very highly in love for their work's sake. Christian servants must work for their masters, even the cruel ones, with submissive, honest, zealous labor (1 Peter 2:18-19). Believing masters must rule without harshness (Ephesians 6:9). Paul does not call for the societal abolition of slavery, but tells Philemon to treat Onesimus like a brother, not a slave, thereby implicitly undermining the institution.

As we can see, a biblical theology of equality shows that equality is a word that cannot be used to mean the same thing in all contexts. Are humans equally in God's image? Yes. Are humans equal? No—not in ability, intelligence, perceptiveness, appearance, or even opportunity.

EQUALITY

Some equality is good and should be fought for: equality before the law and equal access to the Gospel. Some equality is impossible and is like chasing rainbows: equality of outcome for all, equal pay for all people, equal education for all aptitudes, equal roles for different sexes, ages, and abilities.

Some forms of equality are justice. Some forms of inequality require redress to obtain that justice.

Some forms of inequality are not unjust; they are simply the form of creation. Some forms of enforced equality are unjust and produce the very opposite of what they claim to pursue.

6

FREEDOM

Freedom is another word that the disingenuous enjoy. Just as the *tolerazis* cry "intolerance" and pose as victims even while they terrorize and bully others, so similar people shout *freedom* while insisting that others submit to their choices, or at least abdicate legitimate authority over them.

Freedom has a nice ring to our ears. *Restraint* and *submission* do not - at least on this side of the Garden. *Freedom* comes to our minds with almost unquestioned innocence—as if freedom is always the better part that the wise and enlightened choose.

For those who prefer darkness over light, defining freedom is an annoyance. They would prefer a sentimental attachment to a vague notion. But if we walk in the light, as He is in the light, we will quickly see that freedom is related to something outside itself. If you are free, you are free *from* something, *and* free *to do* or *be* something. So, when people tout their freedom, the first question to ask them is, "What have been freed from?" followed by, "What have you been released to do?"

Most have not thought of *free* as a word requiring modification. For them, it means something like, "any sense of burdensome restraint has been lifted from me" or "permission to do all I want." It is similar to their definition of love, which to them means "giving me permission to do what I want without judging me."

The same inchoate, garbled articulations of freedom are found in the church. They emerge in defenses of pet sins: "I'm free in Christ; you can't bring me back into bondage!" They appear as attempted excuses for rebellion: "I don't have to live under the bondage of this authoritarian, mind-controlling legalism. Grace has set me free!" They even posture as theological: "We are not under the Law anymore! We must enjoy our liberty!" These represent nothing more than a Christian adoption of the secular idea of freedom, while giving it a (tacky) theological gloss.

Freedom or liberty might be properly defined as freely choosing to do what one ought. The various kinds of freedom – religious liberty, political liberty, individual liberty – are still applications of this idea. This definition is inescapably grounded in a transcendental view of reality. Liberty, in its complete sense, is composed of two parts: the free choice, and what the free choice is for. *Oughtness* can only be defined by an appeal to human nature, which is an appeal to natural law and divine revelation. What we ought to do is what is good for human flourishing, what is in accord with our created nature, what corresponds to the Divine intention for man. These can only be determined by appealing to the court of Design: what man is and what he was made for.

Defining what we ought to do based on modern bureaucrat-speak is an exercise in circular definition, or nonce-speak. *Progress, community-building, interests of society, healthy societies, harmony* are all words that attempt to hide the essential need for values to rest on ultimate ideas. Progress towards *what*? What should a community, when *properly built*, look like? What exactly *is* in the interest of society? What constitutes *health* in a society, and what does the diagnosis of societal sickness contain? Around what kind of unity should society's members harmonize? Of course, secular bureaucrats and educationists will never attempt to answer these questions, for it would impale them upon the sharp edges of some religious definition of reality, which they scrupulously avoid. But unless we define what man *ought* to do, we cannot define what he should freely choose. Liberty is inextricably linked to human nature.

According to this definition, freely choosing to do what one ought *not* to do is a move towards tyranny or anarchy. Freely choosing sin or evil is an exercise of liberty, but it is also an *abuse* of liberty, and, therefore, an incremental *surrender* of liberty. In the created order, abuse of liberty cannot go on indefinitely without enslaving the one abusing it. This is Paul's point in Romans 6: whatever we freely yield to becomes our master. The tyrannical master of sin curtails our liberties until we find ourselves unable to freely choose anything but sin. The anarchical nature of a depraved human nature means that the liberty of sin is a nightmarish nihilism, a torturous chaos, a quicksand of corrosive pleasures. "While they promise them liberty, they themselves are slaves of corruption; for by whom a person is overcome, by him also he is brought into bondage." (2 Peter 2:19)

Mastery by Christ brings the liberty of continued submission: "I love my master; I will not go out free." (Exodus 21:5)

SOCIETAL AND INDIVIDUAL FREEDOM

Liberty is the absence of unwarranted coercion, leaving the human open to persuasion and his own agency to choose what he ought. Freedom does not, and never can, mean an unlimited number of choices. The freedom of a man should be limited in two ways.

Externally, he is not free to harm the common good, which is decided by the society in which he lives. When a man screams about his "rights" and his "freedoms" while his actions are illegal according to the law of the land, he is head-butting the rockface of Reality. Freedom does not mean complete permission to perform everything that comes into one's head. The Western idea of freedom means freedom to own property, travel, assemble, trade, vote, defend oneself, worship, and express an opinion without coercion or fear of prosecution, within the bounds of the law. Those freedoms, established by centuries of statecraft and jurisprudence, constitute one's freedom in society.

Counterintuitively, at this level of human life, these freedoms are protected by *force*. The policeman's gun, the judge's gavel, and the prison-warden's keys insist that humans use their freedoms within the boundaries established by law. This coercion is not tyrannical as long as it is upheld by the rule of law, limited government, and fair courts. Government is established by God for the health of a society, and the closer the government represents those ideals, the freer the society. In such a society, a man who crosses the boundaries of his legal freedoms forfeits his freedom. He will be coerced into paying some kind of penalty. But wailing that his freedom has been violated when he is led off to prison after the due process of the courts is mangling the meaning of freedom.

But that is not the end of it, for a second consideration should limit a man's freedoms. *Internally*, he should be constrained by devotion to God – by the pursuit of an upright conscience. In any society, that means plenty of choices are externally "legal," while being morally wrong. On the other hand, a healthy society can only survive when the external order is built upon the internal moral order of its citizens. Citizens who pursue what is impure, wasteful, destructive, or defiling simply because it is not forbidden to society, are enslaving themselves and contributing to the overall loss of freedom for society.

A Christian must reckon his range of choices to be those belonging to newness of life and reckon himself dead to sinful choices. Of course, he can exercise his free agency to sin, but this means he is re-entering the tyranny of sin. To maintain liberty, he must restrict himself to all those choices found in the will of God. So ironically, the freest man is the one who limits himself to the will of God and the law of the land (assuming those laws are just and the government is not tyrannical). By limiting his range of choices to what is tolerated by his society and, further, what is pleasing to God, he is the freest man of all.

Why then do we hear so many people yelping about their freedoms being denied, and quoting Galatians 5:1 out of context? With their vague view of liberty, just about any annoyance can be construed as infringing on one's freedom. What then constitutes genuine loss of legitimate freedom?

On the external, societal level, when a government legislates matters that should be left to private choice, liberty is curtailed. The restrictiveness of the laws and the severity the punishments for breaking them is the measure of the oppressiveness of the society, and any move in this direction is a movement towards tyranny.

Conversely, the society that does not uphold the rule of law, that permits bribery and corruption, or allows wanton wastage and destruction of natural resources is headed for the opposite bondage of anarchy. These represent genuine losses of freedom.

On an internal level, as we have said, moves towards sin are moves toward both the anarchy of sin and the tyranny of the flesh, the world and the Devil. These represent a self-chosen loss of freedom.

What is left is to consider when internal matters of conscience become matters of coercion, rather than persuasion. This what most people are talking about when they say they are "free in Christ" or that their legalistic church is busy enslaving people. What does a loss of legitimate freedom look like in the church, that voluntary organization that is to respect the individual conscience? That deserves a section of its own.

FREEDOM AND CHURCHES

A church is a voluntary society. Baptists believe that people join churches not by birth, but by choice. People freely associate and can freely disassociate with a church. Voluntary societies cannot use force or coercion on their members; they can only persuade.

Having said that, a number of things need to be said to overturn the muddled thinking about liberty in Christ and "legalistic" churches. A voluntary organization or society can define the rules of association as narrowly as it wants to. Depending on the nature of the organization or institution, it may not be wise to make those rules of association extremely rigid. But as long as people freely associate or disassociate, no one's freedom has been harmed. Anyone who joins an intensely narrow church does so under no compulsion. If you voluntarily join a church or attend an institution which contains practices or beliefs that you know will violate your conscience, you cannot then claim that you have been oppressed or had your freedoms removed.

Voluntary societies do not have to tolerate what secular society tolerates. Because everyone is freely joining, voluntary societies can exclude plenty of behaviors and beliefs which they find intolerable and include others they find desirable or even essential. They can make intolerable behavior unacceptable in written rules (however many they wish – hundreds, perhaps); they can form a church covenant to which members vow to pursue faithfulness; they can form a simple or detailed statement of faith and insist that members believe every sentence or agree with it in spirit. They can remove people from their membership (so long as due process is followed) for failing in these practices or dissenting in belief. What they cannot do is break the law of the land (insofar as it is consonant with God's law) or go about such removal in a way that violates other Scriptures. None of this, in principle, violates anyone's freedom. We might critique a church or institution for being overly rigid, unnecessarily exacting, or extremely narrow in its tolerance. We could equally critique the individual voluntarily submitting to such a church. But, if people can freely join and freely leave, no one can accuse that church of being tyrannical or of bringing people into bondage.

With that in mind, we can refute a number of calumnies commonly thrown at conservative churches.

It is not coercive authority to teach God's Word with well-warranted application, however detailed or practical it might get. Working God's Word into areas of music, dress, entertainment, leisure, alcohol, use of technology and ethical matters is no violation of anyone's freedom. Issues of conscience are not off-limits to the pulpit, as long as the teacher makes it clear that such is what they are.

It is not coercive authority for a church to discipline someone for verified, unrepentant sin, nor is it coercive to discipline someone who has left. Surely, the objector argues, there is no reason to discipline someone who no longer attends. This objection misunderstands what church discipline is for. It is not to "get someone out," though the removal of a divisive person may be one of its forms (Titus 3:10). The primary function of church discipline is to rescind the church's acknowledgement of a person's faith and baptism and end its covenant with that person. This may take place even when the person continues to attend and certainly takes place if he or she has left. No one is "controlling" the individual in question – he or she is free to disassociate. But it is the mentality of a spoiled child to insist that churches must not discipline those who have left. Indeed, this would be curtailing a legitimate freedom of the local church – to receive and remove members.

Assuming that sin leads people into deeper bondage, faithful preaching and discipleship is not coercive, but liberating. What then would be genuine coercion and tyrannical leadership in the church?

First, if pastors lead through force and not persuasion, this is coercive behavior. Peter describes this behavior as the opposite of leading through servant-like example and teaching, but by acting as overlords who dominate through the sheer force of their position and personality (1 Peter 5:3). Diotrephes is certainly an example of this the kind of tyrannical leadership that Peter forbids (3 John 9-11). If members are removed by the fiat authority of the pastor, if a bully-pulpit shames and intimidates, if emotionally childish games of shunning and chumming train the members to comply, this falls short of the freedom required of a local church.

Second, if the church's statement of faith, covenant or constitution is altered without the consent of the church, this is coercive behavior. Since these are the basis of the voluntary association, to alter them without congregational consent is to lord it over the people of God. If a pastor begins to disagree with these statements, he ought to offer his resignation. If the church body requests that he remain and teach his dissenting views, it can then decide whether to accept his resignation or change their founding documents.

Third, if the pulpit stealthily extends what is fundamental to the voluntary association of the church, this is coercive behavior. Now, in healthy churches, it is inevitable that the pulpit must teach more than what is contained in the church's founding documents. Here the pastor will seek to persuade through the force of sound exegesis and clear reason. However, if the church does not embrace such teachings or practices, it is a matter of failed persuasion – not a matter of a member violating the church covenant. The pastor cannot enforce additional beliefs or practices as essential to church membership; to use the measures mentioned above is tyrannical.

Fourth, if matters of conscience are taught as if they are clear commands or prohibitions, the freedom to judge has been curtailed, and this is coercive behavior. These matters of conscience deserve a full section of their own.

MATTERS OF CONSCIENCE AND FREEDOM

Scripture devotes two sections of the New Testament to explain how certain choices in the Christian life are not explicitly or implicitly forbidden or prescribed: explicitly by commands or prohibitions, or implicitly by a very clear application of general Scriptural principles. These two sections are Romans 14, and 1 Corinthians 8 to 10. Here we meet matters sometimes called *adiaphora* ("indifferent things"). Specifically given as examples of *adiaphora* are eating food offered to idols, and the observance of certain days. Modern Christians have, perhaps without warrant, classed many other things as examples of adiaphora: entertainment, dress, recreation, drugs and alcohol, language, and even sexual purity. Since, in the minds of some, these then become examples of "liberty," and any questioning of them becomes some form of legalism, bondage, or narrowness, it is worth debunking some evangelical haziness about adiaphora.

ADIAPHORA ARE NOT "EXTERNALS"

This is a quick-'n-easy term for lazy minds who prefer to abbreviate judgment into split-second intuitions. Nothing about adiaphora clearly makes them something *external* as opposed to *internal*, whatever the proponents might actually mean by that vague categorization. This unfortunate and unhelpful dichotomy probably comes from misinterpreting Christ's words in Mark 7:14-23, where He explains that the defiling matter is not the food that goes into the body, but the sin that emerges from the heart. I once heard a theological dabbler tell a room full of people involved in Christian radio that this Scripture means that the music that goes in our ears can never defile us; only our hearts' reactions can defile us. I wanted to ask if that holds with watching pornography, but all the heads nodding around the room told me that a lot of ears were getting a pleasant scratch at that moment, and my interruption would hardly go down well. Clearly, the point of Christ's words is not that anything we take into our eyes or ears is incapable of defiling us. The point was to teach some Pharisees that foods declared unclean were not intrinsically evil, and that the far greater moral danger lay within. At any rate, if we are to keep this ridiculous external/internal method of dividing up the Christian life, there is very little that I cannot happily lump with the less important "externals": what I watch, listen to, wear, eat, drink, where I go, what I buy, how I spend leisure time. Pretty soon, what is genuinely "internal" is conveniently a closely guarded-secret: my thoughts about God, or my Gospel-centered meditations.

What's going on here is that a generation of Fundamentalists made lists of rules regarding dress, makeup, theaters, haircuts, beards, and rock music, and the children of those Fundamentalists are now responding with their much shorter two-column list. As silly as some of those lists may have been, and as ridiculous as it was to dictate to everyone's conscience, this does not mean all of previous Fundamentalism was "external," and that the prodigious present generation have newly discovered "internal" Christianity. Rather, what we should hope to say is that while the previous generation often attempted to define the boundaries of their movement by dictating what the conscience should believe, the present generation is attempting to teach sound judgment for the conscience. That might be wildly optimistic, but it's a better articulation of the issue than this silly and unhelpful internal/external dichotomy.

ADIAPHORA ARE NOT MEANINGLESS

It is common for people freewheeling in their thoughts about matters of liberty to say that *adiaphora* refer to matters without any meaning or moral significance. They like to say that these matters are "morally-neutral." But this is impossible because in God's universe everything that exists has a meaning. And since it is meaning-laden, it is not amoral. In a personal, moral universe, there is a sense in which molecules, galaxies, sound waves and scents are moral. In a second sense (the sense that the proponents probably mean it), objects or potential actions which are not intrinsically morally defiling or edifying can become instruments of moral action by humans. What Romans 14 and 1 Corinthians 8 to 10 teach us is that some objects or actions do not have a fixed morality pertaining to their use. In other words, while there is a command, "You shall not steal," there is no command, "You shall not eat food offered to idols." Instead, the action of eating food offered to idols requires careful judgment. In some circumstances, it is wise and permitted; in others, it is unwise or even forbidden. It can be used both ways, but once used, the action is either sinful or obedient. It is certainly not meaningless.

ADIAPHORA ARE NOT ALWAYS UNIMPORTANT

Though the Greek term *adiaphora* ("indifferent things") might lead us into thinking we can be *indifferent* to their importance, this is not the meaning of the term. In Greek philosophy, the *adiaphora* were those matters that could not be *differentiated* into either good or evil. This did not make them unimportant, merely difficult to classify or judge. Some Christians infer that clear prescription or prohibition in Scripture indicates a priority to God, while an apparent silence proves an indifference, or lack of concern, on God's part. While it is fair to say that what is essential will be communicated in the Bible, and what is non-essential will not, this is a far cry from saying that a lack of explicit Scripture on a topic indicates it is of little import. This reasoning would make most ethical matters (abortion, bioethics, the environment, the death penalty, etc.) unimportant. Simply because a matter requires that we use careful, critical judgment in the absence of explicit commands or prohibitions hardly makes a given matter unimportant.

THE ROLE OF *PREFERENCE* IN *ADIAPHORA* MUST BE PROPERLY DEFINED

Proponents of this phraseology, "preference-issue" or "matters of preference" suggest that matters of conscience are determined by the internal likes or dislikes of the Christian in question. Now, it is true that when we have eliminated the forbidden and the unwise, and remain uncertain on the best or wisest choice, we must do what we think is best. But by this definition, *preference* is simply good judgment – thoughtfully parsing meaning so as to glorify God. If this is how we define "preference," well and good – let preference guide. But what some people mean when they tout *preference* is that we should determine these matters merely by what we arbitrarily like, what tickles our fancy, what amuses or pleases us, and that such pleasure or displeasure has no moral significance, like choosing between red and blue. But this misses the real point: *why* does something please you, and *should* it please you? If you bother answering those questions, then you mean *preference* in the first, good sense: good judgment. If you don't ask those questions, then what you mean by *preference* could be defined as prejudice, whimsical inclinations, or merely appetites. And I hardly think Paul would summarize Romans 14 or 1 Corinthians 8-10 with the words, "Look, in these areas, just do what feels good, you know?"

JUDGING AREAS OF FREEDOM

Modern Christians are in the habit of labelling all sorts of things as "matters of Christian liberty" or "areas of preference." We do not doubt that these *adiaphora* ("indifferent things") exist; Scripture explicitly deals with them in Romans 14 and 1 Corinthians 8-10. The question is, how do we identify them?

Genuine *adiaphora* can be identified by a process of elimination. Anything explicitly commanded or prohibited is clearly not an area of liberty. Further, anything forbidden or commanded by a more general principle cannot be an area of liberty either. If we can supply good and clear warrant for connecting a Scriptural principle to a practice, we no longer have an area where Christians may have opposite convictions, and both be pleasing to Christ.

After this process of elimination, what will remain are those matters where multiple principles of equal weight seem to apply, some of which seem to point in opposite directions. In these cases, no Scriptural principle will clearly take precedence over another. Further, the information we obtain from the world to understand this practice may have meaning on various levels. Here is where careful judgment must take over. Among the questions we will ask are:

1. How is this thing typically used? What activities, actions and ends is it used for?
2. Does it make provision for the flesh (Romans 13:14)? Are you fleeing from sin and lust by doing this? (2 Timothy 2:22)?
3. Does it open an area of temptation or possible accusation which Satan could exploit (Ephesians 4:27)? Are you taking the way of escape from temptation by doing this (1 Corinthians 10:13)?
4. Is there a chance of enslavement, or addiction (1 Corinthians 6:12)?
5. Does it spiritually numb you and feed the flesh or worldliness within (Romans 6:12-13)?
6. Does it edify you (1 Corinthians 10:23)?

7. With what is this thing or activity associated? Does it have the appearance of evil (1 Thessalonians 5:22)? Does it adorn the Gospel (Titus 2:10)?
8. Could an unbeliever or another believer easily misunderstand your action? Does it lend itself to misunderstandings (Romans 14:16)?
9. Could your action embolden a Christian with unsettled convictions to fall back into sin (1 Corinthians 8:7-13)?
10. Could your action cause an unbeliever confusion over the Gospel or Christian living (1 Corinthians 10:27-28)?

If two Christians seeking to please God could answer the above questions honestly and yet differently, we have a genuine area of liberty.

But notice, we have not here been agnostic about meaning. Instead, since the area is neither explicitly commanded nor prohibited, we have been especially scrupulous with meaning. The example which Paul uses in 1 Corinthians 8-10 shows us that the focus for *adiaphora* is not the preference of the person, but the *meaning of the situation*. Paul teaches that the solution for *adiaphora* is a careful judgment of meaning. These are not areas of freedom to do whatever appeals to you. These are areas in which all Christians have the freedom to judge carefully, and then obey that judgment (1 Corinthians 10:25, Romans 14:20, 22-23).

Having been careful with our inner judgment, we are then to be charitable with others who have followed the same process and come to different conclusions. In particular, Romans 14 calls on believers to neither despise nor judge one another when we come to opposite conclusions. Further, the strong are to bear with the weak. Who then are the weak?

The weaker brother is not always the "stricter" brother. By this logic, every move towards permissiveness would be a move toward maturity. To abstain from some practices hardly makes one weak in conscience. Someone strong in faith may have a particularly "strict" conviction relative to another believer.

The weaker brother is not the more easily offended brother. This brother is simply the *crabbier* brother. He is a brother who takes personal offense where he should not and needs to be discipled in the virtues of forbearance and patience.

The weaker brother is the brother whose conscience has not settled, who is prone to falling back into a pattern of sin. He is tossed to and fro in his understanding of the *adiaphora*. He may find refuge in extreme denials and abstinences, but he will just as quickly fall back into foolish indulgence. His weakness is not his abstinence, nor his thin skin. His weakness is his lack of stability in judgment and the volatility of his conscience. This brother, whose conscience is wobbly and unstable, is to be carefully guided by those Christians whose consciences have settled. They are to limit themselves, sometimes denying their own freedoms, to protect the believer from unwise or foolish choices while he cements his convictions.

7

HATE

Hate has become the only sin the left recognizes. To them, it is apparently not possible to sin sexually, and any and every form of sexual sin is to be celebrated publicly. Slaughtering innocents (perhaps the most heinous form of murder) is to be cheered and encouraged. Stealing other people's property is no sin if it is "redistributing" or "redressing inequality." No authority or family bond is sacred; any and all of them can be dissolved in the name of statism, equality, tolerance or climate change. Lying and distortion have become commonplace. And what passes for arguments for "better living standards for all" or "the top 1% paying their fair share" is nothing more than coveting your neighbor's goods. Those are commandments five, six, seven, eight, nine, and ten that you can break with no guilt or regret.

But there is one sin, and it may be unpardonable. *Hate* is the sin that the left regards as the chiefest of evils. If your words can be classified as hate-speech, you can be jailed. If your actions can be construed as a hate-crime, you will be facing the wrath of the law. If the courts don't nab you, general society will. You may be called a hater, a bigot, a racist, a Nazi, and many other unpleasant things before you have even had the chance to tell your apoplectic neighbor that you actually love him or her.

What is this sin of hate? Asking the question of your accuser may bring a momentary puzzled silence. Hate has become a catchall word for *opposition*. Whether you oppose something the left cherishes in a quiet, private way, or in a loud, public way, it will be considered hate. Whether your opposition is a religious belief that something is sin, or whether it is a practical concern with the impossibility of some leftist ideology, it will be considered hate. Whether it is refusing to recognize imaginary genders and use the corresponding pronouns, or whether it is simply insisting that you and your own house regard heterosexual marriage as the only natural way of human sexual relations, it will be considered hate. Whether you defend Christianity against attacks, or whether you evangelize others, it will be considered hate. Opposition is hate.

In other words, there is a Tower of Babel of ideologies. As long as you join and co-operate, you are fine. Bow to the image, burn your incense to Caesar, take the Mark and you're a good, enlightened Christian. As long as you do not oppose any of the popular positions held by the leftist elites, then you believe in *love*. If you actively or passively oppose those positions, then you believe in *hate*. And haters don't deserve civility. That is, haters should be hated.

HATE

The childish partiality of this use of "hate" is transparently obvious for any with eyes to see. But for a Christian, the word *hate* has more complexity. After all, there are several Scriptures that commend hate.

> You who love the LORD, hate evil! He preserves the souls of His saints; He delivers them out of the hand of the wicked. (Psalm 97:10)

> Do I not hate them, O LORD, who hate You? And do I not loathe those who rise up against You? I hate them with perfect hatred; I count them my enemies. (Psalm 139:21-22)

> The fear of the LORD is to hate evil; pride and arrogance and the evil way and the perverse mouth I hate. (Proverbs 8:13)

> Hate evil, love good; establish justice in the gate. It may be that the LORD God of hosts will be gracious to the remnant of Joseph. (Amos 5:15)

> If anyone comes to Me and does not hate his father and mother, wife and children, brothers and sisters, yes, and his own life also, he cannot be My disciple. (Luke 14:26)

> But this you have, that you hate the deeds of the Nicolaitans, which I also hate. (Revelation 2:6)

Granted, *hate* does not refer to the same thing in all those verses. But that is just the point. Scripture clearly has kinds of hatred that it commends and kinds that it condemns.

> Hatred stirs up strife, but love covers all sins. (Proverbs 10:12)

> Now the works of the flesh are evident, which are: ...idolatry, sorcery, hatred... (Galatians 5:19-20)

So should we hate, or should we not? Is hate an Old Testament phenomenon? If we are to hate, what kind of hate is "righteous hate?"

To repair this mangled word, we should begin by finding out what kind of hatred God condemns. Second, we should investigate the kind of hatred God Himself exhibits and therefore expects his people to have. Third, we should understand how a right hatred affects our understanding of love, including love for our enemies.

THE HATE THAT GOD HATES

God does not hate all hate. Some hate is actively encouraged by God. Indeed, if hate exists as the opposite of love,

HATE

it follows that, in many cases, we must hate the opposite, or the destroyer, of what we love.

Some hate, however, is condemned by God. In the following verses, hate is the opposite of righteous behavior:

> Consider my enemies, for they are many; and they hate me with cruel hatred. (Psalm 25:19)

> They have also surrounded me with words of hatred, and fought against me without a cause. (Psalm 109:3)

> Thus they have rewarded me evil for good, and hatred for my love. (Psalm 109:5)

> Hatred stirs up strife, but love covers all sins. (Proverbs 10:12)

> Whoever hides hatred has lying lips, and whoever spreads slander is a fool. (Proverbs 10:18)

> Better is a dinner of herbs where love is, than a fatted calf with hatred. (Proverbs 15:17)

> Though his hatred is covered by deceit, his wickedness will be revealed before the assembly. (Proverbs 26:26)

> Idolatry, sorcery, hatred, contentions, jealousies, outbursts of wrath, selfish ambitions, dissensions, heresies... (Galatians 5:20)

> For we ourselves were also once foolish, disobedient, deceived, serving various lusts and pleasures, living in malice and envy, hateful and hating one another. (Titus 3:3)

Similar to this negative use of the word hatred is the word translated "malice":

> Therefore let us keep the feast, not with old leaven, nor with the leaven of malice and wickedness, but with the unleavened bread of sincerity and truth. (1 Corinthians 5:8)

> But now you yourselves are to put off all these: anger, wrath, malice, blasphemy, filthy language out of your mouth. (Colossians 3:8)

> For we ourselves were also once foolish, disobedient, deceived, serving various lusts and pleasures, living in malice and envy, hateful and hating one another. (Titus 3:3)

> Therefore, laying aside all malice, all deceit, hypocrisy, envy, and all evil speaking. (1 Peter 2:1)

HATE

The problem with sinful hate is not its negative flavor. All hatred is negative by definition. But if it is the negative form of a good love, then it is not evil. If you love animals, you will hate cruelty to them. If you love creation, you will hate its pollution or destruction. If you love human well-being, you will hate cancer. If you love babies, you will (or you *should*) hate abortion. Hate, like love, cannot be judged in the abstract. Love is only virtuous if its object of its love is worthy. Hatred is only evil if its object is something God loves.

In these verses, malice refers to "a mean-spirited or vicious attitude or disposition, malice, ill-will, malignity" (BDAG). In other words, malice delights in destruction. It does not hate something that is destructive of the one it loves; it hates another and loves its destruction. God does not delight in destruction for its own sake. "'Do I have any pleasure at all that the wicked should die?' says the Lord GOD, 'and not that he should turn from his ways and live?'" (Ezekiel 18:23).

God's hatred is always His love acting against those things or people that corrupt, defile, or destroy His love.

What sort of hate does God then hate?

WE SHOULD NEVER HATE WITHOUT CAUSE

"Let them not rejoice over me who are wrongfully my enemies; nor let them wink with the eye who hate me without a cause" (Psalm 35:19). We know this ugly tendency in our hearts from the earliest age when we develop a baseless antipathy towards another child, or character on a screen. Evil is irrational and does not answer to reasonable explanations. Ask Evil the question, "Why do you hate me so?" and it will reply, "I just do." This kind of irrational, blind, and senseless hatred is hated by God.

WE SHOULD NEVER HATE OUT OF PERSONAL REVENGE

"Beloved, do not avenge yourselves, but rather give place to wrath; for it is written, 'Vengeance is Mine, I will repay,' says the Lord" (Romans 12:19). Justice for injuries and evil done to us is a function of human government, not individual vigilantism. On the personal level, we are not to take vengeance on our enemies in our hearts. In fact, we are told to do something both inwardly and outwardly to prevent this. Outwardly, we should meet our enemy's needs if the situation arises (Romans 12:20). Inwardly, we must avoid all forms of gloating and delighting if our enemy suffers (Proverbs 24:17-18).

HATE

WE SHOULD NEVER HATE WHAT GOD LOVES

Included in the things that God loves are all humans made in His image (John 3:16), the Church (Ephesians 5:25), the people of Israel (Romans 11:28), righteousness and justice (Psalms 33:5), a cheerful giver (2 Corinthians 9:7), and the works of His hands. While we may hate distortions, corruptions, and perversions in something God loves, we may never hate the thing or idea that God loves.

This leads us to the perplexing question about God's love: does God truly love the sinner and hate the sin?

DOES GOD HATE SINNERS?

God's hatred is a necessary part of His love. Whatever opposes, harms, defiles, or otherwise threatens what He loves, experiences His displeasure, often erupting in righteous indignation: a divine demand for change. We could say that God's hatred is an ally of His love, destroying those things which are destructive of the true, the good, and the beautiful. People who love what God loves are told to hate what He hates, which includes those who hate Him (Proverbs 8:13; Psalm 139:21-22).

God hates several things: pride, lying, murder, evil thoughts, evil inclinations, bearing false witness, sowing discord among brethren (Proverbs 6:16-19), formalistic worship masking wicked living (Isaiah 1:14), idolatry

(Deuteronomy 16:22), and divorce (Malachi 2:16), amongst other things. In fact, most every reference to something or someone being "an abomination to the Lord" refers to something that is loathsome or detestable to Him, a strong indicator of His hatred.

But the thorny question is this: does God hate individuals? Could a God of love hate people?

A plain reading of Scripture seems to indicate that, at least in some ways, He does. God is said to hate all workers of iniquity (Psalm 5:5) and everyone who is wicked and loves violence (Psalm 11:5). God told Israel that He hated the nations He was casting out before them (Leviticus 20:23). God said to Hosea that He hated Ephraim (Hosea 9:15). He loved Jacob and hated Esau (Malachi 1:3-4). Even where the word for hatred suggests something weaker than antipathy, one can hardly doubt that God directs this affection towards individuals and groups of people, not merely actions.

How do we reconcile God's love for all men (John 3:16; 1 Timothy 2:4) with His apparent hatred of people? One common suggestion is that the Bible is merely referring to God's hatred of the person's *actions*, where the action and the person are identified as one, but only the action is meant. But this only raises another question: can one make a sharp distinction between the sinner and his sin? And, more importantly, does God do so?

While it could be plausibly argued that an omniscient God is able to perfectly separate the sinner from his sin, the real question is whether God seems to do so in Scripture. On the contrary, Scripture often speaks of sinners and their sin in the same breath (Romans 1:29-32; 2 Timothy 3:2-5). God's wrath rests on both the sin (Romans 1:18-23) and the sinner (Romans 1:24-32). Furthermore, God does not send sin to Hell; He sends sinners there. It was not merely man's sin in the abstract that was punished on the cross, it was Christ the Person suffering as the substitute for persons who are sinners. As someone said, "There is no abstract sin that can be hated apart from the persons in whom that sin is represented and embodied."

While a distinction between sinner and sin is a handy one for protecting the individual from God's hatred, it simply cannot bear up under the weight of Scriptural evidence which has God showing hatred, or wrath, resting on individuals. Jesus condemns people as workers of iniquity (Luke 13:27) and will take personal vengeance on those who reject God (2 Thessalonians 1:8). Deuteronomy 28:63 describes God's joy in destroying those who are disobedient, which would be very hard to square with the idea of God hating the sin but loving the sinner. Even secular psychologists report a general difficulty with the idea of separating sin and sinner.

A more satisfying answer as to how a loving God can hate individual sinners than the division between doer and deed is to say that human beings are more than one thing. They are sinners, to be sure, but they are also made in God's image (James 3:9; Genesis 1:26). Insofar as the imago Dei is never erased, God cannot completely abhor the individual human. Augustine, when dealing with almsgiving, came close to this idea: "So then, we are not to support sinners, precisely insofar as they are sinners; and yet because they are also human beings, we must treat them too with human consideration."

In other words, what it means to be God is to be able to love and hate sinners simultaneously. We'll consider this possibility next.

GOD LOVES (AND HATES) YOU

Does God hate the sin and love the sinner? We have seen it is more biblical to say that God both loves and hates the sinner. Several theologians have suggested just that.

Augustus Strong wrote, "These passages show that God loves the same persons whom he hates. It is not true that he hates the sin, but loves the sinner; he both hates and loves the sinner himself, hates him as he is a living and willful antagonist of truth and holiness, loves him as he is a creature capable of good and ruined by his transgression."[1]

D. A. Carson put it thus: "Thus there is nothing intrinsically impossible about wrath and love being directed toward the same individual or people at once. God in His perfections must be wrathful against His rebel image-bearers, for they have offended Him; God in His perfections must be loving toward His rebel image-bearers, for He is that kind of God."[2]

Even John Calvin saw that both were possible. "All of us therefore, have that within which deserves the hatred of God. Hence, in respect, first, of our corrupt nature; and, secondly, of the depraved conduct following upon it, we are all offensive to God, guilty in his sight, and by nature the children of hell. But as the Lord wills not to destroy in us that which is his own, he still finds something in us which in kindness he can love."[3]

The best way to harmonize the biblical evidence is to affirm that God is able to love and hate a sinner at the same time.

---

[1] Augustus Strong, *Systematic Theology*, vol. 1 (Philadelphia: The Judson Press, 1907), 290.

[2] D. A. Carson, "God's Love and God's Wrath," *Bibliotheca Sacra* 156 (October-December 1999), 389.

[3] John Calvin, *Institutes of the Christian Religion*, vol. 2, bk. 2, trans. Henry Beveridge (repr., Grand Rapids, MI: Wm. B. Eerdmans Publishing Co., 1994), 435.

Of course, this solution raises its own questions. If God is infinite in His essence and immutable as to His nature, then each of His attributes, including love or hate, must be infinite and without growth or diminution. How then could God love sinners infinitely and hate them infinitely at the same time? To love and hate a person infinitely would seem to cancel each other out. Further, are we to assume that God has the same infinite love and hatred for a believer that He has for an unbeliever, or for Satan himself? How was Daniel "greatly loved" (Daniel 9:23) more than anyone else? To summarize the questions, if an infinite God loves and hates at the same time, how can there be any degree to His love and hatred of individuals, as various Scriptures seem to suggest is the case?

The best answer is that a person can be more or less identified with his sin. This is probably the idea behind John's statement that "he who is born of God does not sin" (1 John 5:18). One born of God is not thoroughly identified with sin as a practice, even though he still sins (1 John 1:8–10). Once justified, the believer is more identified with Christ than he can ever be with the old detestable nature. Justification locates a sinner in the center of God's pleasure: His Son. God may be angry with a justified sinner for his sin, but Christ's intercessory work means that the child of God is ever accepted in the Beloved (Ephesians 1:6). Indeed, progressive sanctification apparently moves one in the direction of ever-opening vistas of knowing the love of God, precisely because one is becoming more identified with what God loves (Ephesians 3:16-19).

On the other hand, an unregenerate person may be on a trajectory that drives him ever deeper into union with his sinful nature, making his sin and his person increasingly indistinguishable. He does not simply commit sin; he delights in it (Romans 1:32). There comes a point when people are guilty of such "extended, hardened, high-handed lovelessness" of God, that they come under a curse. When one thinks of extreme examples of human evil like Hitler, Stalin, or Pol Pot, one does not find it hard to consider their very persons as hateful because they have become so identified with their evil deeds. To take it one step further, very few people shrink at the idea that God hates Satan. This is probably because Satan is so closely associated with his evil, that, in his case, to hate the sin and the sinful being are almost the same thing.

God's infinite love for His own image within human beings and His infinite hatred of sin in them means He cannot grow in love or hatred towards humans. Thus, is not to suggest that God's love does not truly respond to human behavior. Instead, the trajectory of sinners towards sin or away from it drives them to be more or less identified with God's wrath. God's infinite love or hatred does not change, but as sinners move in respect to His holy nature, they are more or less identified with His hatred.

Finally, as Stephen Charnock put it, "Punishment is not the primary intention of God." God's hatred only functions to preserve what He loves. Though God's love is infinite, He values some things more than others. Uppermost in His affections is His own glory. Therefore, if sinners become so identified with their sin that they stand fundamentally in opposition to God's glory, God's love for His own glory will manifest itself in punitive hatred for those sinners' rebellion, more so than in His love for His remaining and marred image in those sinners. Indeed, a marred mirror of God is at one and the same time a cause for love and anger in God.

THE COMPLEXITY OF HATING WHAT GOD HATES

No one should love what God hates. No one should hate what God loves. But, as we have seen, God has the ability to love and hate at the same time. It is this conscious simultaneity that we lack and which adds such difficulty to our understanding of hate.

We have seen the kind of hate which is forbidden: irrational, baseless hate, personal animosity or malice, and hatred of something precious to God. We have seen some of the hates commanded by God: hating evil, hating God-hatred, hating false doctrine. Our difficulty is how to prevent holy hatred from becoming evil hatred; how to maintain a hatred for what God hates, while still loving what God loves.

We can picture the problem in thinking how to view a particularly heinous human being. If we imagine, say, an unrepentant child abuser, we should feel revulsion towards his acts. We should desire that his cruelty and selfish exploitation of the ignorance of little ones be stopped and stopped permanently. We should desire a retribution commensurate with his crime.

But all this is true because, unexpectedly, we still love him. We love the image of God in humans, and for that very reason, we demand that the man live up to that. We are angry exactly because he is not an irrational animal, and we expected him to behave humanely to other humans. Our demand for justice would be meaningless were he incapable of responsible choice but is fitting precisely because we still think of him as human. Our love for him as a neighbor demands we do anything but dismiss him. We may punish him, incarcerate him, or execute him, but in each of these acts, we treat him according to his rank: an image-bearer.

Here is where we can see the great lovelessness of much modern secular thought, particularly on the Left. In attributing moral evil to psychological derangement, by explaining sin as a necessary result of environmental factors, by calling evil a "sickness" or "disease," they do not love our neighbor more, but less. For to the degree that we remove moral culpability from an adult, we remove also his humanity from him. The less responsible a man is, the more he moves towards the beasts and away from the angels. By excusing his sin with his genes and his biology, we have not liberated him, we have made him a slave of physical forces. By calling for *rehabilitation*, we are not offering a cure, but imposing a life-sentence with the same sin. By insisting that society "tolerate" his sin and referring to those who don't as "haters," we handcuff the man to his evil with the golden chains of society's approval.

Christian love is real love precisely because it accords rank and dignity to humans and makes consequent demands upon them. The applications for Christians are obvious. We may feel revulsion, anger, distaste, and indignation towards moral sin and evil in the world. We are supposed to hate those things and feel indignation that an image-bearer of God is deepening his union with rebellion against God. We can only do that, though, because we retain love for our neighbor. We believe "he is as we are" and believe that he may, by the saving grace of God, leave corruption and embrace life.

Because we are also progressively being changed into Christ's image, we should be aware of how imperfectly we perform this love and hate. Our moral outrage is quickly mixed with personal annoyance, pride, jealousy, revenge, malice, and haughtiness. This does not mean we should abandon the enterprise of loving what God loves and hating what God hates because we are likely to introduce sin. It means we attempt to be angry without sinning, without letting the sun go down upon our wrath (Ephesians 4:26). It means we consciously think of ways to display love to our enemy, to overcome what would become fleshly malice, if left to itself (Romans 12:19-21).

In fact, the most difficult love command is the command to love our enemies, for here love and hate meet in the same person. The Lord Jesus' only explanation for how and why to love our enemies is simple: God also loves them and meets their needs, ungrateful as they are. "For He makes His sun rise on the evil and on the good and sends rain on the just and on the unjust." (Matthew 5:45). We are to love people who hate us or hate what we love—even while we hate their hate and, possibly, hate what they love. And we should expect that it will take growth and struggle to achieve this.

We are naive if we imagine that the world will understand this love and its concomitant hate. Theirs is a binary formula: niceness to all and fury upon all who do not show niceness to all. Self-contradictory as it is, it is not open to reason. It may, however, be persuaded by beauty: "Having your conduct honorable among the Gentiles, that when they speak against you as evildoers, they may, by your good [beautiful] works which they observe, glorify God in the day of visitation (1 Peter 2:12). They will likely slander all acts of judgment, discernment, and thoughtful discrimination as malicious hate, and they will likely not honor acts of love for what they are. Since that is the case, Christians should get on with loving what God loves, hating what God hates, and proving to the world that Christian love alone brings peace on earth and goodwill to all.

"HATE" — A WORD LIKE "ATHEISM"

His name was Polycarp, and he was a disciple of the apostle John. He later became the pastor of the church at Smyrna. When he was very old, the vicious persecutions of Christians in Smyrna turned on him. He was arrested and told to deny Christ. He refused. He was brought into the stadium to be killed before the audience of unbelievers.

The governor looked down on him and said, "Consider your age, and be sensible. Swear and say, 'Down with the atheists.'" Polycarp looked at the pagan audience in the stadium, and said, "Down with the atheists." The governor said, "Swear, reproach Christ, and I will release you." Polycarp answered, "Eighty and six years have I served him, and he never once wronged me; how then shall I blaspheme my King, who hath saved me?"

Polycarp's dialogue with the governor requires a bit of commentary to be understood. When the governor told Polycarp to say, "Down with the atheists," he meant for

Polycarp to renounce Christianity. *Atheist* was a pejorative term that pagans threw at Christians. To a polytheistic society awash in gods, goddesses, temples, and all their paraphernalia, Christianity seemed, at first glance, a religion of denial. They denied these gods existed and denied the reality behind the statues and figurines. To pagans, the Christians were unbelievers, deniers of their gods. They were atheists, not in the modern sense of the term, as materialists or naturalists, but as those who refused belief in the gods.

Of course, to Christians, the real atheists were those who denied the existence of the one true and living God: the triune God of Scripture. To fail to believe in Him is to fail to believe in the only God who exists. Pagans were the true atheists. Polycarp's response was dripping in irony. He repeated the precise words required of him, but everyone understood that he meant the opposite of what they intended him to declare. Pagans called Christians, *atheists*. Christians denied the charge and called the pagans, *atheists*.

Perhaps something similar is happening today with the word *hate*. Unbelievers are very free with the word *haters*. Christians, particularly those of the conservative kind, are said to be haters. Why? They do not endorse homosexual marriage. They do not recognize transgender pronouns. They do not accept Islam as a road to reconciliation with God. They hold to the Bible as God's Word. This makes them purveyors of hate, people without tolerance, acceptance, and affirmation.

Christians would deny that charge, as we have done in this book. We would explain our understanding of love, hate, and tolerance. We would affirm that we pose no physical threat to those who differ with us, nor are we disturbers of the peace. Conversely, we might counter the slander with a question: who are the real haters? If people vandalize our businesses, make false allegations about Christians being elected to high office, pour vitriol of the most unsavory kind upon us in print and in person, and attempt to limit the exercise of free speech among Christians, should we call these people *tolerant* of Christianity? Should we say they are *open and affirming* of our beliefs? Should we say they practice *inclusivity* when it comes to Christianity? No, we will say, at least among ourselves, that they appear to hate what we believe and stand for.

And there the impasse will remain. I doubt that Polycarp convinced pagans to stop calling him an atheist while they remained pagans. He understood their blinded condition and simply taught who were the true atheists and the true worshippers.

I doubt we will convince the rabid left that Christians are not haters while they remain committed to their radical notions. Best to recognize their blinded condition, and keep teaching who truly loves, and who is practicing real malice.

HATE

Perhaps one day, if you are a Christian, you will be called by some authority and told to say, "I renounce all bigoted, intolerant and hateful forms of speech and religion." With Polycarp, wave your hand at the assembled unbelievers and say, "I renounce all bigoted, intolerant and hateful forms of speech and religion."

8

RELEVANCE

Perhaps one of the great put-downs today is to be told that your church is not *relevant*, or that your preaching is not relevant to "the issues people are facing." Being called *irrelevant* cuts a little deeper than being called *intolerant*; for if you're cited for being intolerant, it merely means your teaching may have hit a nerve; whereas, being called *irrelevant* is to be dismissed as useless, with a casual wave of the hand. We can handle having opponents to our view; being sloughed off as unneeded and unwanted is harder to stomach.

But as we keep listening, we soon realize that the word *relevant* has near-infinite flexibility in the minds of its abusers. Some mean something like "current." Something is relevant if it represents what is novel, or contemporary. Relevance means something like what is currently being said, done, or used. Promoters of this meaning of relevance have a snobbish disdain for anything older than, say, the year of their birth. What's new is true, what's true is new, and, therefore, whatever is familiar is what is relevant.

Others, when speaking of relevance, have a vague notion of a something like importance, or value. Relevance is a measure of importance, even of urgency. Something is relevant if it has enough weight or force to merit attention, and if something is irrelevant, then it no longer carries enough weight to demand our attention.

For others, *relevance* carries the idea of practical value. The relevance of something is measured in terms of tangible effects and results. If it can achieve whatever end was set out for it, then it is relevant; if not, it is simply irrelevant. Similar to this, some think of relevance as intelligibility. If it seems too cerebral and abstract, it becomes, to them, irrelevant.

Still others think of relevance in terms of notoriety. If one has celebrity status (famous for being famous), thousands of followers, or some kind of fame, then one has consequent relevance. By implication, the anonymous and little-known must be, well, *irrelevant*. What is widely known is often widely loved, and so whatever is relevant must simultaneously be appealing to as many people as possible.

Smuggled into this mangled use of "relevant" are a lot of assumptions. One is that the chief end of man is to appeal to his current generation's lusts and appetites. A second is that the dead have nothing valuable to say to the living, and that the current generation represents the furthest man has come and the best he can be. A third is that if we focus mostly on means, the ends will take care of themselves, that instruments are more important than ideals. A fourth is that fame and power are forms of value that are necessary to a life of eternal significance.

These, and others, will be our delightful duty to demolish, to restore a sane and thoughtful use of the word *relevance*.

RELEVANT OR CURRENT?

When some people speak of the importance of *relevance*, they don't mean relevance at all. After all, *relevant*, strictly speaking, merely means "pertinent to the matter at hand." Relevance needs an object: relevant to whom or what matter? we may ask.

The fact that some people use the word *relevant* as a quality not requiring modification demonstrates that they really mean something else by it. One particular usage is perhaps the most common: describing whatever is current as "relevant." If something is current, it could have several qualities. It could be something currently in use. It could mean it is a new development. It could mean it is fashionable, trendy, in vogue. It could mean it has been adopted by the youth, the trendsetters, the celebrities (those famous for being famous). Yet all of these share one unquestioned value for the relevance-devotees: they are new. In the mind of relevance-devotees, novelty is always good.

Ours is a world where "new!" on the product's packaging boosts sales. "Brand new season" is supposed to invite wide-eyed excitement. "Never before seen" is a declaration of greatness. We check our phones for updates hourly. We want to know the latest. News that is "breaking" is important. "A new development" in the story is supposed to firm up its sagging relevance. This is the age where the new is true, and the true is new. Only the recent is decent.

We shouldn't be surprised. If Darwinism is true, then the latest development is always the most advanced. If science is man's savior, then the newest gadget is necessarily the best. In such a world, you are permitted to say these words with a sneering disdain: *old, tradition, custom*.

The logic behind equating relevant with current contains three premises.

1. We need to bring practical value to this world.
2. What is of practical value to this generation must be current.
3. We are only relevant to the degree we are current.

With some qualification, the first premise is hardly objectionable. The second is the most problematic, but it represents the spirit of the age. Our culture practices chronological snobbery, a term coined by C. S. Lewis and defined by him as, "the uncritical acceptance of the intellectual climate common to our own age and the assumption that whatever has gone out of date is on that account discredited."

Lewis goes on:

> You must find out why it went out of date. Was it ever refuted (and if so by whom, where, and how conclusively) or did it merely die away as fashions do? If the latter, this tells us nothing about its truth or falsehood. From seeing this, one passes to the realization that our own age is also "a period," and certainly has, like all periods, its own characteristic illusions. They are likeliest to lurk in those widespread assumptions which are so ingrained in the age that no one dares to attack or feels it necessary to defend them.[1]

The Christian view of reality in considerably different. The fifth commandment itself, in commanding reverence and obedience to parents, is implicitly demanding respect for the past: honoring the accumulated wisdom of one's parents gained in the decades they are in advance of oneself. And, to be sure, their wisdom was not self-taught, but came from their parents, who received some from theirs, so that we find that the command to honor one's immediate parents is really a command to honor one's ancestors. God's people were even to honor ancient

---

[1] Lewis, *Surprised by Joy*, Kindle, loc 2540.

landmarks, to rise in the presence of the aged, to regard the gray head as a sign of gathered wisdom. So convinced were the Jewish people of the value of tradition, that Christ had to confront them with their unwarranted obedience to man-made traditions. This seems a far cry from modern evangelicalism, with its anti-traditional tradition.

While no Christian would argue the importance of bringing value to the world, a Christian steeped in Scripture recognizes the difference between what is *permanent* and what is *current*. Permanent things may or may not be currently popular (2 Timothy 4:2-4). But what is true, good, and beautiful is permanently pertinent to the life and well-being of a creature made in God's image. Something current, on the other hand, may be one of countless spasmodic experiments in novelty that a godless culture will produce. The church that weds itself to a particular generation will find itself a widow in the next. Nothing is as irrelevant as a trendy church.

Those who build with gold, silver, and precious stones, are permanently relevant. Those enamored with the wood, hay, and stubble of the fashions of the day, may find little is left of their ministry at the Judgment Seat of Christ.

RELEVANCE

RELEVANCE AND IMPORTANCE

When some people speak of "making Christianity relevant," they are referring to demonstrating Christianity's importance and applicability. They fret over the fact that unbelievers and the wider culture dismiss Christianity and religion so easily. Secularism provides people with enough food, shelter, conveniences, comforts, and sufficient diversionary amusements to keep them morally anesthetized from the pain of contemplating ultimate questions. Today's secularist finds it all too easy to ignore questions of eternity and Christ, an attitude which was less common in previous generations, which felt their mortality more acutely. When noticing the disturbing ease with which unbelievers ignore God, some Christians feel that "the church has become largely irrelevant" and that it must "establish its credibility and demonstrate its *relevance* to unbelievers."

Here is a jumble of truth and error. On the one hand, it is clearly true that few ages in world history have possessed such irreligious attitudes. Today, you can grow up in a secular culture and live most of your life feeling that religion is a strange practice performed by strange people. It is undeniable that the average secular unbeliever does not see how church, Scripture, or worship is germane to his life. In that sense, the things of God indeed *seem* irrelevant to him.

On the other hand, the Bible explains this phenomenon. It does not say that the fault is with the church for failing to contextualize the Gospel adequately by adopting every available cultural form to clothe the gospel in. Instead, it describes human beings as intractably set against the lordship of God. Romans 1:19 explains that the knowledge of God is part of created human nature. John Calvin put it this way, "There is within the human mind, and indeed by natural instinct, an awareness of divinity. This we take to be beyond controversy. To prevent anyone from taking refuge in the pretense of ignorance, God himself has implanted in all men a certain understanding of his divine majesty."[2]

What does man do with this knowledge? Verse 18 tells us. He suppresses it. What dictators do with bad press is what the human heart does with continual evidence that God is, and God is a judge. Secularism just makes it easier for people to do what they have always preferred to do: ignore God.

In other words, the problem is not that an unbeliever cannot see how Christianity is relevant to him, as a result of some inadequacy in Christianity itself or of the way it is proclaimed. The problem is that a man cannot see Christianity's relevance after deciding that he *will not* see its

---

[2] John Calvin, *Institutes of the Christian Religion* (Philadelphia: Westminster Press, 1960), 43, 45-46.

relevance. This is a willful overlooking (2 Peter 3:5), a chosen rejection, and a blindness by shutting one's eyes. And if this natural, stubborn blindness isn't enough, Satan compounds this with added blindness (2 Corinthians 4:4).

When a man is blind, we don't speak of making potentially dangerous obstacles in his path *relevant to him*. They *are* relevant to him! Given his propensity to injure himself by walking into them, nothing could be more germane, important, applicable, or relevant to him than those obstacles. A neighborly thing to do would be to tell the blind man what he's about to walk into.

Christianity does not have to be *made* relevant. It *is* relevant. Nothing is more relevant to a creature made in God's image than his standing before his Creator. Matters of life, death, eternity, goodness, evil, justice, and the soul are relevant to every man. Christians cannot make these things more relevant to a man than they are. We can only speak of them clearly and live soberly and righteously in this present age. The Holy Spirit is the only one who can change a person's perception of the message from foolishness to wisdom (1 Corinthians 1:18).

Having said that, there are ways that the church can make the message of the Gospel seem *less* relevant. When it clothes its message in trendy slogans and commercial schtick, it appears as if it is one more product being marketed. When it uses entertainments and amusements to create interest, it appears as if its message is weak and in need of marketing props. When it tries to appear wise and noble in the world's eyes (or cool, hip, trendy, sick, or whatever the current word is), it appears as if it is a sycophant of the world, limping between two loyalties. All of this shouts louder than words can say, "Yes, unbeliever, your dismissal of God is justified and normal! We, too, are bored with the plain Gospel! But look! We have some shiny attractions which we'll give you, if you deign to patronize us with your attention!" Instead of confronting the believer with his moral rejection of God, we treat his sin as natural and normal, and beg him to come for other reasons. Christianity does not become less relevant when Christians act this way, but it does compound the problem by giving unbelievers even more hardness to their hard hearts. The unbeliever intuits, "The Christian doth protest too much." Such ways and words do not sound much like Paul:

> For I am not ashamed of the gospel of Christ, for it is the power of God to salvation for everyone who believes, for the Jew first and also for the Greek (Romans 1:16).

RELEVANCE AND INTELLIGIBILITY

Modern Christian champions of *relevance* mean many things by the term. One use is the concept of intelligibility. When calling for the church to be relevant to this generation, they mean that its message must be understandable, clear, and intelligible.

Thus far, no objection. No command exists to make the gospel obscure or arcane. If the Christian message is to be applied to anyone's life, it is necessary that it be intelligible.

But it is at this point, as Christians think about not only communicating accurately but *successfully*, that many a Christian takes his eye off the ball, and the meaning of relevant shifts from *intelligible* to *plausible*.

Intelligibility and plausibility are related, but quite distinct. When something is intelligible, it can be understood by the average, rational human. When a matter is intelligible, nothing is incoherent, garbled, or indecipherable to an average intelligence. Plausibility refers to how likely something is to be true. It describes something qualitative: how believable something seems to a person. Why something is plausible to a given mind has to do with many things, not all of which are related to its intelligibility: the presuppositions or worldview in place, the inclination of the heart, and the often-unrecognized motives and desires. We find something plausible both because of what we think *could* be true, and because of what we desire *would* be true (or untrue, as the case may be).

When churches do not make this distinction, they can make critical errors in evangelism, missions, and discipleship. Making the Christian message intelligible is a question of good communication. Making the Christian message plausible to an unbeliever is a question of moral persuasion. The Christian message is relevant, so therefore it ought to be made intelligible. But its relevance does not always mean it will be plausible.

Christians should seek to persuade. Paul certainly did. At the same time, Paul made it clear that certain forms of persuasion were morally unacceptable.

> But we have renounced the hidden things of shame, not walking in craftiness nor handling the word of God deceitfully, but by manifestation of the truth commending ourselves to every man's conscience in the sight of God. (2 Corinthians 4:2)

> For we are not, as so many, peddling the word of God; but as of sincerity, but as from God, we speak in the sight of God in Christ. (2 Corinthians 2:17)

"Craftiness," "deceit," and "peddling," all speak of methods of persuasion that are manipulative, deceptive, or subversive to the Gospel.

Manipulative techniques get one to decide in favor of the message through the introduction of other motives: fear, guilt, or carnal lusts, just to name three. Manipulative altar calls, appeals to self-preservation, or desires for wealth and comfort may be persuasive, but they fail as Christian forms of communication.

Similar to manipulation is deception. The idea that the Gospel message can be hidden, or smuggled in, while masquerading as another message is deceptive. Clothing the Gospel in popular entertainments, games, amusements, and other pleasures, so as to insinuate its message, is deceit. Paul refused to persuade through deception and insisted on being open about his motives for preaching the Gospel.

Finally, if the message is subversive, it undermines the meaning of the Gospel while simultaneously claiming to promote it. By appealing to sinful desires, endorsing worldly attitudes, or encouraging what the Gospel saves us from, such a presentation subverts the entire message of the Gospel.

When some Christians say the gospel must be relevant, they mean using, as John MacArthur lists it "staged wrestling matches, pie-fights, special-effects systems that can produce smoke, fire, sparks, and laser lights in the auditorium, punk-rockers, ventriloquists' dummies, dancers, weight-lifters, professional wrestlers, knife-throwers, body-builders, comedians, clowns, jugglers, rapmasters, show-business celebrities, reduced length of sermons, restaurants, ballrooms, roller-skating rinks, and more."

None of this will make the gospel relevant. In a twisted way, it will make the gospel seem more plausible to those for whom it is foolishness. But the irony is, by trying to make the gospel plausible to those for whom it is foolishness, the church must use—yes, you guessed it—foolishness. This, in turn, makes the users of foolishness...fools. Paul chose to be a fool in the world's eyes, by preaching the wisdom of God, rather than a fool in God's eyes for preaching the wisdom of this world.

RELEVANCE AND NOTORIETY

One of the powerful spells cast over the modern world is the charm of celebrity. Someone quipped that a celebrity is someone who is famous for being famous, but few stop to notice that. Celebrity culture is the true opiate of the masses, and if it were not so, the word *paparazzi* would never have become an English noun.

Celebrity culture assaults us everywhere: advertisements using celebrities to hawk their products, reality talent-shows with the "prize" of becoming a "pop idol," magazines unashamedly titled "Vanity Fair," and click-bait links to online tabloid-gossip. Most mainstream news sites have an entire section devoted to the habits and happenings of celebrities, just to be able to compete with other news outlets.

RELEVANCE

Fame is an unquestioned good in our society. In premodern times, fame was accorded for outstanding accomplishments: the Roman general, the philosopher, the inventor. Today, you can become famous for being famous.

Added to this soul-sickness is the idea that everyone can and should seek fame. Self-promotion is no longer frowned on as vanity; it is become a quite acceptable, and even required, social behavior. The preposterous poses of many a Facebook profile display the utter shamelessness and unselfconscious egotism of a person in "I'm a celebrity too" mode. All that posing and lip-pouting is just tongue-in-cheek, of course; except that it's not. Just a few decades ago, such peacock-strutting would have been considered pathological.

Much of this is the fear of anonymity. Ironically, the Internet has not created a "global community" as much as it has intensified the sense that you are just one soul among seven billion strangers. Perhaps like never before, a sense of significance is only achieved when some kind of notoriety is gained. Becoming a celebrity, even if for a few moments, lends some meaning to the chaos, and some weight to an otherwise weightless life. To avoid the pain of anonymity, you need to *be someone* (as if you are not anyone, until many other people know you). Everyone understands that to *"be someone,"* you must become notorious.

A church captive to the culture is just as charmed by celebrity. This is hardly a new development. Tozer wrote this over fifty years ago: "We swoon over celebrity. Whatever they say, we accept as the important word for the day, even if it goes contrary to plain biblical teaching. St. Ignatius said, 'Apart from Him, let nothing dazzle you.' But we allow everything but 'Him' to dazzle us these days. We have become rather bored with God and the truths of Scripture."[3]

Christians are just as interested in the antics of the famous godless. Witness how sweaty-palmed Christians become if a famous sportsman, actor, tycoon, or media personality openly admits some kind of faint affinity to Christianity. A near stampede breaks out to have the celebrity come and "give his testimony" in church. Why the raised pulses and bated breath? Because if a famous person endorses Christianity, that will surely show how "relevant" it is to the average man.

Of course, when we can't entice or pay an unbelieving celebrity to patronize Christianity, the next best thing is to create our own, right? Evangelicals are happy to then create their own superstars: usually pastors of large churches, with their own TV shows, podcasts, syndicated radio shows, thousands of Twitter followers, and plenty

---

[3] A. W. Tozer, *The Dangers of a Shallow Faith: Awakening from Spiritual Lethargy* (J. L. Snyder, Ed.; Regal: Ventura, CA, 2012), 31.

RELEVANCE

of book deals. Let's not forget our musicians: if pagans can have rock stars, so can we. And what do we do with our celebrities? Conferences, of course. We use their names and faces on the posters, draw the crowd, and celebrate our celebration. That way, we're displaying our "relevance," particularly to the youth. (Hard not to laugh at the consternation of the Christian hooked on celebrity culture when he moves out of his ghetto for a day and finds that most people have never heard of his stars. "John who? Who's he?")

What has relevance to do with celebrity? Nothing at all, rightly defined. The importance and practical value of something is not determined by how popular or well-known it is. Seasons in Israel's history show that truth is sometimes a minority report. Church history shows the same. Scripture even seems to suggest that mass appeal may be a sign of error and looming destruction (Luke 6:26; Matthew 7:13). Confusing relevance with celebrity would be to confuse widespread evangelism with mass influence or political clout. It assumes that what is well-known among the populace will have moral traction and influence upon them. Therefore, to this thinking, Christians must become celebrities or find celebrities who will endorse them. Evangelicalism has been doing this since they days of Billy Sunday.

Christianity is no less relevant if it goes into near eclipse. Christianity remains relevant whether it is in season, or out of season. Christianity is relevant if all the world rejects it, yea, *Athanasius contra mundum*. Christianity will be relevant if God continues to call people who don't qualify as celebrities:

> For you see your calling, brethren, that not many wise according to the flesh, not many mighty, not many noble, are called (1 Corinthians 1:26).

RELEVANCE IN THE EYE OF THE BEHOLDER

A book on chastity may not seem *relevant* to teenagers necking in a parked car. First-aid kits don't seem *relevant* to two boys beginning a scuffle. Wedding vows don't appear *relevant* to a person plunging into an affair. When we are morally committed to a course of action, it narrows the horizon of what we see as important, practical, or useful.

We live in a culture which is furiously committed to sexual perversion, to a life of diversionary amusements, and to the accumulation of creature comforts. Avid participants in this culture will have a very different view of relevance to that of a faithful Christian.

For a Christian, relevance is determined by a permanent standard: what pleases God as revealed in Scripture. This standard is nuanced by our historical understanding of the Christian faith. With this in place, a Christian rejects several mangled forms of the idea of relevance.

First, relevance is not determined by how current or novel something is. The idols of contemporaneity, "progress," and innovation have no intrinsic purchase on whether something is valuable, useful, or pertinent. To equate relevance with novelty is a sub-Christian understanding of the world.

Second, relevance is not determined by how popular and useful something seems to a generation wise in its own eyes. If Proverbs teaches us anything, it is that fools feel quite justified in their self-destructive path and openly scoff and mock the way of wisdom.

Third, relevance is not determined by how easily understood and plausible something seems to others. A lack of spiritual understanding is charged as spiritual dullness and immaturity, not as a faulty message or failure to connect.

Fourth, relevance is not determined by how notorious and famous something becomes. The cream rises to the top, they say, but so does the scum. When all men speak well of you, you are in mortal danger, said Jesus.

A Christian understands relevance because he understands what man is, and what man is for. If you understand man as a creature made by and for God, you can understand what has, as Webster's defines it "significant and demonstrable bearing" on his existence.

In this sense, relevance is determined by whoever is making the judgment. If the beholder is an unbeliever committed to self-rule and self-indulgence, you can be sure the claims of Christianity will seem "irrelevant" to him. Our goal is not to "make Christianity relevant" to him. Our goal is to show him his whole concept of what is valuable is skewed and rebellious. In other words, the only way for a rebel to consider Christianity relevant is if he becomes, by regeneration, a worshipper.

9

TASTE

De gustibus non est disputandum, said the ancient Romans. *There is no disputing over taste*, meaning that, in matters of personal taste and preference, there can be no profitable dispute, and, therefore, there ought to be none.

There's much truth to that. If you're a fan of murder mysteries, and have no time for fantasy, then we have no quarrel. If you're partial to Elgar instead of Bach, then live and let live. If seafood floats your boat, and red meat turns you off, then to each his own. Jack Spratt could eat no fat, and all that.

The problem with the word *taste* is that it refers to more than one human experience or ability. Because we use the same word for these quite different things, we run the risk of equivocation: speaking in two voices. We may mean one thing but seem to mean the other. We may find ourselves alternating between the two meanings in the same conversation. This not only brings confusion to discussions, it can also be manipulated by the dishonest. To heal this mangled word, we need to separate the competing or differing meanings and find synonyms to use alongside *taste*.

The first meaning is the one meant in the Roman maxim. Here, taste refers to individual preference. The creation is awash in a variety of colors, tastes, fragrances, textures, sounds, shapes, words, ideas, and the infinite combinations thereof. Part of the variety is the individuality of the human being, who at the earliest age begins to demonstrate preferences, likes and dislikes. Differing tastes encourage more variety, more experimentation, and more innovation. It is in this sense that the phrase "beauty is in the eye of the beholder" is loosely true: individual preference finds pleasure where others do not.

Within the sphere of what is upright and pleasing to God, differing taste ought to be a source of curiosity, enjoyment, and fascination. Learning what another enjoys in something I do not will either initiate me into beauties and pleasures I had not known, or at least fill me with new regard and enjoyment of another fascinating human made in God's image. Scripture certainly encourages believers to show deference to one another's preferences, when those preferences fall within the bounds of what is pure, true, just, upright, noble, virtuous, lovely, etc.

The second meaning was very far from the minds of the Latin creators of that maxim. *Taste* in this second sense was used from around the seventeenth and eighteenth centuries to describe a faculty of judgment. Philosophers and aestheticians of the time were grappling with the question of the subjective and variable experience of beholders and the properties of what is beheld. The question of "good taste" and "bad taste" became an important one, even to skeptical empiricists like David Hume. Here *taste* does not refer to preference, but to discernment. As a trained palate can distinguish subtle flavors, so a person of good taste can distinguish between appropriate and inappropriate, beautiful and gaudy, classy and tacky, art and kitsch. The mark of one who has learned and absorbed the accumulated good judgments of thousands of people who have now already died, is that he is "civilized," "cultured," "a man of discrimination," "a man of good taste." The fact that you can already hear the watchdogs against elitism barking after that last sentence tells you all you need to know about the current attitude towards these ideas.

But in fact, Scripture has just as much to say (in fact, much more) on this second meaning of taste. It does not use the term *taste* (just as it does not in the first meaning). It uses the terms *discernment, judgment, wisdom, understanding,* and *conscience.* It gives rather elaborate instruction on how to cultivate this kind of taste, how to use it and not abuse it. And in fact, this kind of taste can only develop through some kind of "disputing." Comparison of judgments, disagreement, discussion, and debate is how these judgments are formed, shaped, chastened, and refined. To fail to compare, criticize and communicate about these judgments is to leave them in the dark, unwatered, and away from sunlight.

Our study of this word will require a few steps. First, we'll need to understand where taste as personal preference is encouraged and protected in Scripture. Second, we'll need to become alert to how this matter of preference is applied in illicit ways in the modern church. Third, we'll need to understand how taste as good judgment is commanded and commended in Scripture. Fourth, we'll need to see how good judgment is developed both in the world and in the Word.

PROTECTION OF PREFERENCE

Scripture loves unity among the saints but does not mandate uniformity. Somewhere Tozer points out that a hundred pianos all tuned with the same tuning fork will all be in harmony with one another. Just so, believers, when conformed to Christ and submitted to the same sound doctrine, will find their Spirit-given unity (Ephesians 4:3).

But within the Body of Christ, we will necessarily be different from one another. Indeed, as unpopular as it might be to say this out loud, we will not even be equal. We will be different in both the degree and the kind of giftedness we possess. We will possess and receive different amounts of honor (1 Corinthians 12:23-24). We will have very different functions in the Body (Romans 12:4).

We will supply different portions of what is needful (Ephesians 4:16). Our differences make us neither useless to the Body (1 Corinthians 12:15-18), nor autonomous and self-sufficient (12:21-22). We are mutually interdependent.

Scripture speaks often on this theme because of equal and opposite errors. One is to expect that unity must flatten out differences and enforce a uniformity of ability, appearance, opportunity or even outcome (as the social justice warriors now demand). This ends up destroying the church's true diversity through legalistic taboos and making unity a matter of outward similarity. The Bible wants us to accept that we are different and yet unified.

The other error is to turn our diversity into a kind of conglomerate of preferences with each competing with the others for its space in the sun. The church becomes a mall of consumeristic "tastes," and everyone demands some shelf-space. Here, preferences turn into protected islands of private property, guarded fiercely, and sometimes even paraded proudly. Here Scripture simply rebukes us for selfishness. A difference in preference can be exploited by the flesh into despising or judging (Romans 14:3, 10). We can parade our preference causing sorrow in another (Romans 14:15). We can flaunt our liberty in front of one whose conscience is still unstable, leading him to choices that will destroy him (Romans 14:13, 20-21; 1 Corinthians 8:7-13). But these are proud responses, selfishly insisting upon our own preference at the expense of another's. Essentially, we assert our differing preference as more important, or more valid, than another's.

This ends up destroying the church's true unity through a foolish tolerance of selfishness, making diversity a matter of mere multiplicity of competing preferences, regardless of how they coexist. The Bible wants us to accept that we are one body, with differences *submitted to that unity*.

Protecting the submitted differences within the church involves several beliefs and practices.

First, believers need to embrace the differences and "inequality" as part of God's created order and redemptive purpose. We do not need to set up quota systems in the church. No one should ever be excluded on the basis of race or wealth or sex. Diversity, when yielded to the lordship of Christ, is beautiful.

Second, believers need to understand the meaning of "the weaker brother." It does not refer to someone with a stricter conviction than yours. Protection of the conscience of others always trumps my own liberty.

Third, believers need to know that liberty is always loving, not self-assertive. The strong protect the weak (Romans 15:1-2). Personal rights and privileges can and should be suspended, delayed, or forgone entirely for the sake of winning others and upholding a blameless testimony (1 Corinthians 9:1-27).

Fourth, believers need to understand that certain areas of life allow for opposite conclusions and practices by Christians, with both sets of Christians pleasing God (Romans 14:5-6). Certain matters can legitimately have more than one approach by very different Christians, and these responses can all be acts of holiness. Identifying and distinguishing these from matters of clear moral prescription or prohibition is where we now turn.

PREFERENCE AND ADIAPHORA

God reveals His will in Scripture in three ways.

The first is by explicit command or prohibition. God simply mandates certain behaviors and forbids others. The second is by principles. Principles give truths, usually in timeless, axiomatic, or generalized form, which must then be properly connected to the specific circumstances that a believer is in. The third is by allowing areas that He neither requires nor forbids explicitly in His Word. Theologians have called these things *adiaphora*, from the Greek which means "indifferent things." These refer to matters where Scripture has not told us one way or another. Here careful judgment is needed. The meaning of the thing or activity in question must be properly understood, and then linked back to Scriptural commands or principles.

It is this third area that we must understand in order to correctly use the term *preference*. One characteristic of modern libertarian Christianity is its tendency to adopt an inverted legalism. In order to justify its "freedoms," it makes an appeal to the letter of the law. That is, it shaves down the actual obligations of a Christian to explicit positive or negative biblical commands. It wrangles free of the implications of many biblical principles, claiming exemption from them with the post-modern motto: "that's just your interpretation." Finally, when it comes to *adiaphora*, it looks incredulously at the one seeking to form a judgment on any such matter. After all, if God hasn't said anything about it, then the matter is meaningless, morally neutral, and without any serious moral implications. By a weird abuse of *sola Scriptura*, the only admissible judgments are the first category of explicit commands and prohibitions. The rest of life, it seems, does not matter to God. Finally, with rich irony, these legalists brand anyone who offers a moral judgment on any of the adiaphora with the term—you guessed it—*legalist*.

It ought to be obvious to us that God did not aim to write an exhaustive manual detailing His will on every possible event. The Bible would then fill several libraries and be an ongoing work.

It ought to be equally obvious to us that God does want us to glorify Him in every detail of our lives (Colossians 3:17; 1 Corinthians 10:31). He has a perfect will, and He wants us to know it (Romans 12:2, Ephesians 5:16). Therefore, it ought to be plain to us that what God has supplied in the Scripture must be applied to life using information not contained in the Scripture.

Why are Christians so intimidated at the thought of getting grounds to apply a Scripture from outside the Scriptures? Probably because they have confused *sola Scriptura* with *nuda Scriptura*. *Sola Scriptura* teaches that Scripture alone is the final authority for life and godliness. There is no higher bar or court of appeal than the Bible. There we find God's will revealed. No information outside of the Scriptures is to be considered as authoritative as Scripture itself.

However, *nuda Scriptura* is the idea that Scripture can come to us unclothed, apart from the understanding imparted from the believing community of faith and the Christian past, apart from the progress of theology through the centuries, and apart from any other accompanying information from beyond the Scripture, even if it be true and given by experts or authorities in their fields. Scripture's authority becomes limited to the naked black-and-white text, and nothing more than its own explicit applications will be admitted. In supposedly wanting nothing more than the unadorned statements of Scripture to guide his life, such a person ironically destroys the authority of Scripture to speak on life in general. Scripture's protectors become its captors, not merely keeping competitors out, but keeping its own authority locked within the prison of its own two covers.

Most *nuda Scriptura* practitioners are unaware of how inconsistent they are with this attitude. They oppose abortion, but the Bible nowhere explicitly says that the killing of an unborn child is an instance of murder. They oppose taking God's name in vain, but they cannot point to a single Scripture which gives an explicit application of that command. They regard recreational drug use as sinful but cannot find a verse which links drug use to principles forbidding addiction or harm to the body.

And yet they oppose these things. That's because they unwittingly violate their *nuda Scriptura* ethos and supply outside (non-Scriptural) information to make a valid application. They find out from doctors that life begins at conception; they reason that using the actual name of God in an everyday slang fashion is to treat it in an unworthy manner; they find out information on the addictiveness and physical effects of the drug in question. In other words, Scripture does not give them either the application, or even the link to the application. They do, through the use of reason and outside information. We do this all the time, and God expects us to do so.

I think the disingenuous attitude of "the Bible doesn't say that" really begins once a cherished idol is under fire. The person lives by *sola Scriptura* in every other area of his life. However, should one of his loves be challenged—his music, his entertainments, his dress to worship, his use of disposable income, his reading matter—suddenly he reverts to *nuda Scriptura*. Now he wants the Bible to speak explicitly to the matter under question, or his supposed devotion to chapter and verse will throw it out. This is a lying heart.

Adiaphora are not areas where the lordship of Christ does not apply, to be exploited for our own convenience. All of life is to be lived for the glory of God, including those areas where Christians can come to opposite conclusions.

PREFERENCE AND AMORALITY

Adiaphora (indifferent matters) are misunderstood on two grounds. First, evangelicals misunderstand the term *indifferent* to mean *unimportant*. Second, evangelicals conflate the moral neutrality of *adiaphora* themselves into *morally neutral actions* once they are used.

First of all, "indifferent things" has nothing to do with feeling indifferent about a matter. *Adiaphora* does not mean "matters of little consequence." The term originates from ancient Greek schools of thought, where it referred to the inability to differentiate two things logically, or the inability to differentiate whether morality demanded a thing or forbad it. In other words, the "indifference" was not a feeling of apathy or boredom with the issue. It had to do with the difficulty of differentiating, not with the unimportance of the issue.

Indeed, consider how formative are those matters which are commonly considered to be preference. Music shapes character and forms the Christian imagination. The observance of days of worship or rest has profound effects on our godliness. Food and drink can be used for asceticism, gluttony, drunkenness, and broader immorality. Forms of recreation, leisure activities, what we watch and listen to, the places we frequent, the clothes we wear, may indeed be matters of preference. This hardly makes them inconsequential for godly living.

Second, "indifferent" things do not remain morally neutral once used by a moral agent. Certainly, food by itself does not commend us to God one way or another (1 Corinthians 8:8). The kingdom of God is not eating and drinking, but righteousness and peace and joy in the Holy Spirit (Romans 14:17). Yes, the heart is established by grace, not by foods (Hebrews13:9). And yes, what goes into a man does not defile him, but what comes out of his heart (Mark 7:18-23). All of this establishes that certain substances, objects, sounds, periods of time, and places are neither intrinsically good nor evil.

Once used, however, these things become instruments of faith toward God, or unbelief (Romans 14:23b). This is Paul's project in 1 Corinthians 8-10: to show the Corinthians that morally neutral food can be used to glorify God or to please self sinfully. It can glorify God in thankful participation, and it can be used to glorify God in deferential and considerate abstention. It can be used selfishly by eating wantonly in front of a believer whose conscience has not stabilized, and it can be used selfishly by eating in front of an unbeliever who associates the food with idolatry. It can be used selfishly by abstaining with a proud and haughty attitude, or by eating with a scornful, in-your-face attitude. The food itself is simply part of "the Earth which is the Lord's and the fullness thereof." It is what moral agents do with the morally neutral food that makes their action moral or immoral.

The childishness found in evangelical circles is to assume that morally neutral objects, substances, materials, or colors somehow transmute the actions of people that use them into *morally neutral actions*. Yes, not every action carries the same moral weight and consequence. But "whether you eat or drink, or whatever you do, do all to the glory of God" (1 Corinthians 10:31). We may have different preferences on food or days, but we both share the same obligation to convert our preferences into worship. "He who observes the day, observes it to the Lord; and he who does not observe the day, to the Lord he does not observe it. He who eats, eats to the Lord, for he gives God thanks; and he who does not eat, to the Lord he does not eat, and gives God thanks" (Romans 14:6).

Put simply, morally indifferent things almost never translate into morally neutral actions, or morally neutral agents. We are required to take those morally neutral objects and discern their nature, their associations, their use, their dangers, their possibilities. We may find that certain morally neutral things, such as the musical notes C, D, or G, or the chemical substance alcohol (C_2H_6O), are no longer morally neutral once combined into a musical language, or an inebriating drink. To rightly use *adiaphora*, we are to consider a number of questions, mentioned in an earlier chapter in this book.

1. How is this thing typically used? What activities, actions and ends is it used for?
2. Does it make provision for the flesh (Romans 13:14)? Are you fleeing from sin and lust by doing this? (2 Timothy 2:22)?
3. Does it open an area of temptation or possible accusation which Satan could exploit (Ephesians 4:27)? Are you taking the way of escape from temptation by doing this (1 Corinthians 10:13)?
4. Is there a chance of enslavement, or addiction (1 Corinthians 6:12)?
5. Does it spiritually numb you, and feed the flesh or worldliness within (Romans 6:12-13)?
6. Does it edify you (1 Corinthians 10:23)?
7. With what is this thing or activity associated? Does it have the appearance of evil (1 Thessalonians 5:22)? Does it adorn the Gospel (Titus 2:10)?

8. Could an unbeliever or another believer easily misunderstand your action? Does it lend itself to misunderstandings (Romans 14:16)?
9. Could your action embolden a Christian with unsettled convictions to fall back into sin (1 Corinthians 8:7-13)?
10. Could your action cause an unbeliever confusion over the Gospel or Christian living (1 Corinthians 10:27-28)?

In other words, out of the three areas that God reveals His will (commands, principles, *adiaphora*), it is ironically *adiaphora* that require the greatest discernment and the greatest wisdom. Far from being a third-tier, unimportant area of life with little to no moral consequences, *adiaphora* turn out to be areas that will affect vast swathes of our lives and shape us profoundly. Perhaps one of the remaining differences between conservative evangelicals and mainstream fundamentalists is that many fundamentalists still recognize the moral importance of *adiaphora*, while evangelicals insist that matters of preference are to be given little attention.

Indeed, there have been those [fundamentalists] who elevated their preferences to inviolable standards for all. But Romans 14 warned us against this. Yes, there have been those [fundamentalists] who converted their conviction into commandments for others. But Romans 14 teaches precisely the opposite. The abuses of *adiaphora* by those who ignored Scripture's teaching on the conscience does not warrant the current dismissal of *adiaphora* as unimportant and morally inconsequential. They are precisely the opposite.

GOOD TASTE AND CHRISTIAN TASTE

Even atheists used to believe in good taste. The infamous David Hume wrote in his *Enquiry Concerning the Principles of Morals*, "In many orders of beauty, particularly those of the finer arts, it is requisite to employ much reasoning in order to feel the *proper* sentiment; and a false relish may frequently be *corrected* by argument and reflection" (emphasis mine).

Today, it is hard to find a Christian who believes good taste is real, founded on objective realities, and possible to identify. Christians have changed places with relativists and seem to be leading the charge.

T. S. Eliot reminded us that those desirous of good literary judgment need to be acutely aware of two things at once: "what we like," and "what we ought to like." Ron Horton said, "Whereas the immature approve of what they like and disapprove of what they dislike, the mature are able to approve what they dislike and disapprove what they like, or are inclined to like."[1]

Approving what we ought to approve of is clearly Paul's prayer in Philippians 1:9-11. Scripture certainly calls for the development of good taste. "Let all things be done decently and in order" (1 Corinthians 14:40). "Finally, brethren, whatever things are true, whatever things are noble, whatever things are just, whatever things are pure, whatever things are lovely, whatever things are of good report, if there is any virtue and if there is anything praiseworthy—meditate on these things" (Philippians 4:8) "But solid food belongs to those who are of full age, that is, those who by reason of use have their senses exercised to discern both good and evil" (Hebrews 5:14).

Taste, then, is a discipline that can be developed. Taste goes beyond preference, for to call something beautiful is to say more than just, "I like it," but to make the claim public in some way, to call on others to share your evaluation. Differing tastes may correspond to the difference between two sorts of beauty. In other words, bad taste is a taste for bad things, the love of what ought not to be loved.

Taste may even be sinful. Frank Brown, in *Good Taste, Bad taste, and Christian Taste*, suggests four forms of sinful

---

[1] Ron Horton, "Christian Taste and the Art Entertainment World" (Bob Jones University, Greenville, SC, 2017), https://theologyin3d.com/christian-taste/.

taste. First, there is the *Aesthete*, who glories in creation, but not in the Creator. Second, one finds the *Philistine*, who cannot appreciate anything artistic or aesthetic, things which "cannot be translated into practical, moral or religious terms." Third, one meets the *Intolerant*, who elevates his own standards to the level of absolutes. Fourth, there is the *Indiscriminate*, whose radical aesthetic relativism embraces all aesthetic phenomenon without discriminating between the superficially appealing and that which has lasting value.

To even speak of sinful taste is highly controversial in a relativistic age, so a few qualifications are in order. First, taste is rooted in a broader cultural context, and cultures necessarily have differences. (This does not mean they do not share universals.) Second, judgments of taste do not function like logical theorems, valid scientific inferences, or valid moral claims. Taste can, *contra* the Roman maxim, be a matter of legitimate dispute. An element of freedom is built into the pursuit of beauty.

With all that said, some form of consensus should be sought, otherwise no discussions of beauty could take place. How does one explain differing tastes in beauty? I suggest four explanations, which I'll take in turn:

1. Aesthetic Maturity
2. The Prevalence of Kitsch and Sentimentalism

3. Cultural Formation and Deformation
4. Natural Preference

AESTHETIC MATURITY

The idea that one's ability to discern beauty is a discipline that can be practiced is unfamiliar to many Christians. It wasn't always so. Jonathan Edwards wrote, "Hidden beauties are commonly by far the greatest, because the more complex a beauty is, the more hidden is it." Again, even a sceptic like David Hume wrote, "Though the principles of taste be universal, and, nearly, if not entirely the same in all men; yet few are qualified to give judgement on any work of art, or establish their own sentiment as the standard of beauty." So, who is qualified? Hume says, "Strong sense, united to delicate sentiment, improved by practice, perfected by comparison, and cleared of all prejudice, can alone entitle critics to this valuable character; and the joint verdict of such, wherever they are to be found, is the true standard of taste and beauty."

Edmund Burke saw the cause of bad taste as a defect of judgment due to lack of natural intelligence, or a lack of training and exercise in judgment. He added that ignorance, inattention, prejudice, rashness, levity, obstinacy, and all other passions that pervert the judgment, will pervert the ability to perceive beauty. Taste, according to Burke, improves as judgment improves, by growth in knowledge, and better attention to the object, and by frequent exercise.

Taste engages much of the human soul. It perceives, appreciates, and appraises. If so, aesthetic maturity must be closely related to other dimensions of morality and maturity, including responsiveness, wisdom, love, and discernment. An overall maturity of character is related to aesthetic maturity, and the corollary is that aesthetic immaturity is a defect in one's overall maturity.

THE PREVALENCE OF KITSCH AND SENTIMENTALISM

If, as the Greeks said, *beautiful things are hard*, one would expect the mature to be able to patiently and carefully discern such beauties, whereas the immature and impatient will pass them over.

A discussion of taste is one of the most difficult (and unrewarding) ones to have, for most people are unreflective about their likes. "I know what I like!" is supposed to end the discussion, followed up with "different strokes for different folks."

Aesthetic immaturity is one of the reasons for a discrepancy in taste among people. Some have not developed their powers of discernment to approve the things that are excellent (Philippians 1:9-11). A second reason is the sheer allure of sentimentalism in art. Christians who care about truth and care about truthful affections should care about the dangers of sentimentalism.

Art that trades in sentimentalism is sometimes called *kitsch*, for it cheapens the aesthetic experience by giving a shallow substitute. Milan Kundera, author of *The Unbearable Lightness of Being*, wrote this much-cited description of kitsch:

> Kitsch causes two tears to flow in quick succession. The first tear says: how nice to see children running on the grass! The second tear says: How nice to be moved, together with all mankind, by children running on the grass! It is the second tear that makes kitsch, kitsch.[2]

When in the grip of sentimentalism, people are not moved by the beauty of the object, people are moved by how moved they are. They feel deeply the depth of their feelings; they fall in love with their love. The art becomes merely something used to obtain what seems to them a moving experience. The only way this is possible is when the qualities of the object perceived possess only superficial schemas of beauty that are instantly recognizable and provoke familiar emotions. Objects of true beauty resist

---

[2] As quoted by Jeremy Begbie in "Beauty, Sentimentality and the Arts" in Daniel J. Treier, Mark Husbands, and Roger Lundin, eds., *The Beauty of God: Theology and the Arts*, Kindle (Downers Grove, IL: Intervarsity Press, 2007), §475-477.

this treatment; they insist on one's submission to them; they insist on honest scrutiny. Roger Scruton:

> Kitsch, the case of Disney reminds us, is not an excess of feeling but a deficiency. The world of kitsch is in a certain measure a heartless world, in which emotion is directed away from its proper target towards sugary stereotypes, permitting us to pay passing tribute to love and sorrow without the trouble of feeling them.[3]

Sentimental art evades or trivializes evil, presenting a fiction of an unfallen present world, and so allows its viewers to wallow in pleasant feelings. The sentimentalist is emotionally self-indulgent, loving, grieving, hating, or pitying, not for the sake of another, but for the sake of enjoying love, grief, hate, and pity. Sentimental art denies the need for sacrifice in approaching beauty, but in so doing deprives feeling of depth and reality.

Dorothy Sayers called such art "amusement art" and noted that what people get from it "is the enjoyment of the emotions which usually accompany experience without us having had the experience." Nothing in such an aesthetic experience reveals people to themselves; it merely enhances and inflates an image of themselves as they fancy themselves to be.

---

[3] Scruton, *Beauty*, 191.

Real art helps its participants to escape, not from reality itself, but from their own unimaginative experience of it. They are returned more aware, more alive to the profundity of life in God's world. Sentimental art simply gives pleasure with the illusion of true imagination. Its consumers do not escape to reality, for no reality is even depicted. The line between fantasy and reality is blurred.

Real art gives those who receive it a kind of objectification in which they are able to see themselves in perspective. The self and the world are understood rightly. They see people as God sees them, with divine objectivity. Sentimental art is all too human and, ultimately, childish. Its consumers want pleasure without change, an escape from pain and ugliness without altering a thing within. And so they escape into non-existent worlds where they are already experiencing pleasure and existing as beautiful. Sentimental art turns its back on a world it has never known.

The problem is not the symbolism in sentimental art, for all art makes use of the symbolic. Instead, sentimental art attractively packages the world by glossing and varnishing it. It prettifies, delighting with sound, shape, and color in overpoweringly sweet doses. The escape comes through shutting out the reality and then envisaging a world in which its consumers are the heroes, the overcomers, the desired lovers, the powerful, beautiful people. It is a world of man's own making, where everything is selected and placed in one's own interest. Defects are polished and characters flattened lest they evoke pity instead of soothing sentimentality. One quickly recognizes the stereotypes and fills them with the feelings one knows he or she is supposed to have.

For this reason, sentimentality is a form of art hostile to what Christianity purports to teach: a denial of self so as to be able to worship the glory of Another. Richard Harries goes as far as saying that "Kitsch, in whatever form, is an enemy of the Christian faith and must be exposed as such."[4] Kitsch is not only an aesthetic failure, but a moral and spiritual failure, too. Christ's beauty is not a sentimental prettiness, and, therefore, sentimental art has the potential of leading into idolatry. Scruton similarly claims that kitsch is not primarily an artistic phenomenon but a disease of faith.

Differences in taste are explained not only by differing levels of aesthetic maturity, but by the human propensity to prefer what is easy, familiar, and flattering. Here the difference is not mere preference, but whether art will be used selfishly or sacrificially, whether it will be an act of learning or an act of narcissism, whether it will be a childish encounter with ourselves or a receptive encounter with reality. Since Scripture describes man's

---

[4] Richard Harries, *Art and the Beauty of God* (London, U.K: Mowbray, 1993), 60.

propensity for self-deception and his inclination towards self-worship, it is no surprise that sentimental art is popular and that unreflective people consider it their preference.

CULTURAL FORMATION AND DEFORMATION

Taste is never shaped in isolation. We learn to love what we love from our family, our church, our school, and our society. In other words, taste is largely shaped by culture.

Culture can be defined as T. S. Eliot suggested: "the incarnation of a religion."[5] At the heart of any culture is Richard Weaver's "metaphysical dream": an unspoken but ever dominant vision of ultimate reality. From this vision, a culture creates worship, art, jurisprudence, custom, and social order. Quentin Faulkner says that "culture is perhaps best defined as the collective behavior (together with the resulting artefacts) of a society engaged in acting out (symbolizing) its most deeply held and cherished shared beliefs and convictions."[6]

---

[5] T. S. Eliot, *Notes Towards the Definition of Culture* (New York, NY: Harcourt, Brace and Company, 1949), 27.

[6] Quentin Faulkner, *Wiser Than Despair: The Evolution of Ideas in the Relationship of Music and the Christian Church* (Westport, CT: Greenwood Press, 1996), 206.

THE WAR ON WORDS

Understood this way, culture is formative and, in some senses, determinative. As the composer Julian Johnson, puts it, "Culture is not something you choose: it confronts you with an objective force. To be sure, it is a composite product of individual consciousness and is amenable to our own work upon it, but it is far from being a matter of choice. Culture is no more a matter of choice than having two legs or being subject to gravity is; one can no more reject culture than reject electricity or weather."[7]

If culture is formative, much of what is wrongly called "personal taste" is actually shaped by the example of others and exposure to others' loves. Tastes are first received before they are scrutinized or even challenged. People begin their lives as members of a culture and identify with its loves and hates; it is only later that they begin to question if they wish to continue to own all that the culture holds dear.

"Ah!" says the musical and aesthetic relativist, "this just shows that taste has no objective standard! It is completely different from one culture to another, and therefore no taste can be judged to be 'better' than another."

Were humans all still living in isolated folk cultures in which they were united by religion, language, and geographical region, we'd have to consider how different folk

---

[7] Julian Johnson, *Who Needs Classical Music? Cultural Choice and Musical Value*, Edition (New York, NY: Oxford University Press, 2002), 117.

cultures have approached beauty, and how taste should be related cross-culturally. But they aren't. The technologies of mass culture have erased geographical boundaries. All that is left of folk culture are those remnants that have been selected by producers of mass culture to create a new product: a movie about Native Americans, a pop song using Swiss yodeling, or a Disney movie about animals with themes sung in Zulu or Swahili. The truth is, we all live in the world of mass culture. The question of universals between cultures is no longer a major question: we're all in the same culture now. And it's really a non-culture. Christopher Dawson says of mass culture, "The new scientific culture is devoid of all positive spiritual content. It is an immense complex of techniques and specialisms without a guiding spirit, with no basis of common moral values, with no unifying spiritual aim…A culture of this kind is no culture at all in the traditional sense—that is to say it is not an order which integrates every side of human life in a living spiritual community."[8]

What kind of taste does mass culture produce in its members? Faulkner suggests two beliefs.

1. A belief in the individual's right to pursue self-satisfaction, self-fulfillment, and self-gratification.

---

[8] Christopher Dawson, *Religion and Culture* (Cleveland, OH: Meridian Books, 1948), 214.

2. Confidence in the potential of modern science to create for us an ever-improving quality of life, coupled with a fascination with the technology that is the result of modem science.

The kind of taste that most clearly corresponds to the first belief is what we disparagingly call *kitsch* (art that makes us feel good about feeling). The taste most properly aligned with the second belief centers on, in the words of Calvin Johansson, "media, presentation and image." A culture given over to this will be one that emphasizes what is more entertaining, such as exciting images, rather than text. When image dominates in a culture, a religion of the Word suffers.

In such a culture, taste is necessarily deformed, and this deformity is reinforced. Indeed, only the mentality of the marketplace would define taste as entirely a matter of individual choice, like products to be purchased and consumed. Only a member of mass culture would see an eclectic selection of cultural products as "personal style." "The equating of cultural choice with personal style signals the end of an understanding of culture as something related to objective spirit".[9]

Mass culture does not, and perhaps cannot, communicate transcendent ideals. Its art forms, made as they are to

---

[9] Johnson, *Who Needs Classical Music?*, 117.

sustain narcissistic interest, are not capable of sustaining the Christian vision of a holy, glorious, and beautiful God. A culture of easy listening and easy living leads to the atrophy of imagination and to simplistic sentiment.

When people are dominated by the sensibilities of mass or popular culture, it deforms taste in all the directions that Christian aestheticians have warned against: using art instead of receiving it, taking immediate responses as the "truth" of the work, promoting aesthetic relativism, and creating an appetite for narcissistic art.

Differences in taste can certainly be credited to the shaping force of culture. To what extent a person is embedded in in mass culture will have a proportionate shaping influence on his aesthetic taste.

NATURAL PREFERENCE

Why are there such different "tastes" among people? Is the debate over music in worship simply a "preference issue?" Are matters of music, dress, and recreation merely matters of "personal style?" We have tried to sort out the meanings of the word "taste" and have seen two distinct meanings.

The first is the act of judging, or discerning. It is the faculty that can tell good from evil, true from false, and beautiful from ugly. When exercising judgment, we are doing more than privately enjoying personal likes. We are trying to find out what is worthy to be enjoyed, known, and experienced. This is a public judgment, one that is meant to be shared, compared, and criticized by others. It is possible for this taste to be more or less true: to conform to what, according to God, is excellent (Philippians 1:10). That does not mean it will be easy, or that our judgments will ever reach unanimous consensus. Apparently, God built difficulty into the world. The fact that we struggle to learn how to love what God loves is instructive in itself. Perhaps true relationships require real thought and meditation, thorough testing and experimentation.

This judgment should be grown and attended to with the same diligence that we give to growing in moral holiness or in theological knowledge. Our aesthetic maturity is not some extraneous social grace or an elitist boasting point, but a measure of whether we can perceive the world as God has made it. It takes long practice and a refusal to simply choose what is easy and sentimental. It requires a self-consciously counter-cultural posture. But it is as necessary as the other areas of worldliness that we abstain from. Loving beauty is not an optional extra to the Christlike person. Good people do not love ugly things.

The second meaning of "taste" is what is usually meant by "preference": the differing inclinations and interests of people. As bishop Richard Harries points out, "There are many kinds of beauty and whilst all forms will be characterized by wholeness, harmony and radiance, they will have these attributes in different ways."[10] If we then imagine a spectrum of truly beautiful things, we may still expect aesthetically mature people to find differing preferences within that spectrum.

Two caveats are in order.

First, such differences ought not to be termed "personal style," a term which usually refers to an eclectic menagerie of beautiful and ugly, one which is supposedly immune from criticism simply because such a collection represents an individual's choice.

Second, aesthetically mature people will be able to recognize why another object of beauty, while not their own preference, has merit and should be judged to be beautiful, or conversely, disdain an object as unworthy, although it may be preferred by oneself or a close companion. The focus is not on freedom to choose; the focus ought to be on supplying plausible justification for your choices, giving warrant for your loves, not expecting the fact that you love something to be justification in and of itself for that love.

In those Philippians 4:8 areas, there is room for preference, indeed, room for opposing convictions. In what displeases God, there is no preference at all. If God has no taste for it, neither should we.

---

[10] Harries, *Art and the Beauty of God*, 24-25.

In summary, the question of good taste is not a simple one. Aesthetic maturity is needed, but relativism rules the day in our postmodern world. Narcissism, sentimentalism, and kitsch provide an alluring and deforming effect on good taste. This bad taste is widely promoted through the media and structures of mass culture. Preference plays a role in explaining discrepancies over good taste, but preference has a far smaller role than aesthetic immaturity, loyalty to sentimental art, and cultural deformation.

Ironically, as in many areas of Christian growth, it takes the presence of a virtue to spot its absence. You need good taste to spot bad taste. You need good judgment to see the errors of bad judgment. Perhaps then, at the heart of Christian good taste is the attribute of humility: the patient, teachable, childlike spirit that is willing to admit its weakness or ignorance, learn from its betters, and develop the discernment to love what God loves.

10

TOLERANCE

Tolerance, today, means something like *embracing and approving people and ideas without criticism*. The tolerant man is the one who does not merely live peacefully with his neighbor but muzzles any criticism he might have of his neighbor. That's about as close as one can get to defining the modern idea of tolerance because it is more of an elastic sentiment than a clear idea, one which morphs according to the target of its protectiveness, or, as the case may be, its inchoate resentments.

This idea of tolerance is incoherent and not even internally consistent. Why is that?

First, there is no such thing as absolute tolerance. No one tolerates everything. Every society sets limits on its tolerance, and those actions or ideas it finds intolerable, it punishes. Few societies, at least in principle, tolerate murder or treason. No school tolerates all behavior; no employer tolerates all work; no country tolerates all views. When the point of intolerance is reached, some form of coercion follows: a spanking, a jail term, expulsion, public shaming, violence, or even execution. This is simply part of human life. The question before us is, when should we be intolerant?

Second, modern tolerance tolerates only versions of itself. That is, it tolerates only those who have imbibed its idea of tolerance. Any person or group that holds different views on what should be tolerated, and when, becomes a target of its ire. Indeed, Christians who hold to the authority of Scripture soon find that their view will not be tolerated. It is transparent contradictions such as this that the *tolerazis* cannot see: they are viciously intolerant of those who don't embrace their view of tolerance.

Third, modern tolerance cannot distinguish between tolerance and agreement. If one agrees completely with another view, tolerance is not necessary. Tolerance, in fact, requires disagreement to make sense at all. Tolerance involves forbearance with a view as it is expressed, or even with a practice, without resorting to any of the coercive methods that stop it altogether. The modern idea of tolerance insists that one must agree with the view and that disagreement counts as intolerance. To truly tolerate under this regime, only silent disagreement is permitted. Furthermore, publicly defending and arguing for your own view, if it conflicts with others, constitutes intolerance.

Much of this stems from secular relativism. If absolute truth is impossible or non-existent, then every man is right in his own eyes. Consequently, to express disagreement with someone's "personal truth" becomes a kind of violation of his being since it is apparently true only in his being. Once truth has contracted to exist only in individual brains, the only way to protect it is to prohibit public disagreement.

Were we to take this farce to its logical end, we should end all debate, discussion, or dialog. The fact that the *tolerazis* would *disagree* with what I'm writing demonstrates that they must equivocate on the meaning of tolerance.

WE OPPRESSED LEFT-HANDERS

It is becoming abundantly clear to many that the call for tolerance has, in fact, not been a call to tolerate all opinions everywhere, but to express agreement and endorsement of certain groups and positions. The LGBTQ+ community, feminists, non-Christian religions, minorities, or previously oppressed ethnicities are usually those said to be suffering from intolerance from others and requiring greater tolerance from others.

This is a tad disingenuous for two reasons. First, if there were no tolerance of such groups, their voices would not be heard in the media, and their marches would be illegal. They would be in jail or worse, as the non-tolerated often are in despotic countries. Once again, tolerance is not the same as agreement. Christians and non-Christians don't agree on the meaning of life, but our children play in the same parks, and we stand peacefully in the same checkout lines. This is tolerance.

Second, the eclectic nature of the group supposedly needing more tolerance or experiencing intolerance seems suspiciously close to the "List of the Previously Non-Tolerated" produced by liberal Western professors. When Marxism was in the ascendancy, liberal professors classified everything according to class warfare and economic motives. Now the hip rhetoric is to speak of oppression, domination, and "ontologies of violence." All things Western and Christian (and in some cases, white or male) tend to be cast as oppressors exhibiting physical or verbal violence on all things non-Western and non-Christian. The *tolerazis* posture as the champions of freedom for previously oppressed groups, but it is obvious to anyone with eyes to see that the crusade is not so much for freedom for all as much as it is about limiting (or extinguishing) the voice of historic Christian or Western views. The New Tolerance is not for Christians—you've been tolerated long enough, don't you know—it is for those on the "List of Previously Non-Tolerated." But the list is not consistent.

Here's an example. I happen to be left-handed. Now consider just how *oppressed* we left-handers have been, and what sort of *tolerance* we are now entitled to.

First, in almost every language, the word for "left" is connected to ideas of evil, deception, inferiority, or things sinister, while the words for "right" suggest trust, correctness, goodness, or ability. To think of how the rhetoric of violence has used language to prejudice the other ninety percent of the world against us just chills my blood.

Second, many societies have forced left-handed children to write with their right hand (and some still do), telling them that the left hand is the dirty hand, the hand for cleaning oneself. This has caused learning difficulties for many. We've been held back economically to the advantage of the right-handed. I'd be richer right now if it weren't for this economic intolerance.

Third, the world has trampled on our rights, neglecting our needs when it has come to doorhandles, scissors, cars, can-openers potato-peelers, computer mice, and the direction of reading, writing, and books in the West. We have been struggling through a world set up to favor the right-handed.

We left-handers check all the boxes for the "List of Previously Non-Tolerated":

- we are a minority;
- our difference has been historically frowned upon;
- people have tried to change us;
- we have been at a social and economic disadvantage.

To counter the vicious intolerance of left-handedness, and to promote society-wide tolerance of left-handedness, should I not march for left-handed equality? Should there not be a government-grant for left-handers to compensate me for the fact that I cannot cut straight? Should I not lobby to have the terms "in his right mind" or "right-hand man" or "righteous" deemed culturally offensive and examples of micro-aggressions? Can we not classify the term "two left feet" as hate-speech? Should building codes and rezoning laws not be changed to reflect the reality of left-handers entering and exiting those buildings? Should right-handers not become automatically guilty of "handism"—a sin which I, as a left-hander, am completely immune to? Indeed, all right-handers are implicated in this systemic oppression which uses language, the media, and the economy to deny me my rights—my lefts, that is. Should they not contribute to some reparation tax?

Well, this little illustration, as facetious as it is, shows the farce of the New Tolerance. The reason I don't get to do any of those things is that left-handers are manifestly tolerated in the society I live in. I don't need more tolerance, however much intolerance once existed

However many people might think us weird, no one imprisons us or executes us. We're tolerated in a secular society precisely as many of the other groups on the "List" are tolerated. Perhaps some disapproval still exists, but no one, in the society I live in, is expelling left-handers from society itself by imprisonment, deportation, death-threats or execution.

Further, the fact that left-handers don't make the "List" shows that the criteria for inclusion are remarkably flexible and, ultimately, hypocritical. I have a hunch that the fact that left-handers are *truly* representative of every ethnicity, religion, and gender (including white Christian males) might be a reason we don't make the "List." In truth, I don't want to be on the "List"—but I can't see a very good reason, by their stated criteria, that I'm not.

To be clear, tyrannical intolerance is an evil. I am not mocking the genuine suffering that humans have inflicted on each other, or the true oppression (which God hates) that has happened and still happens. Racism, religious violence, or other acts of intimidation are evil, and Christians must shun them. What deserves our scorn is the hypocritical New Tolerance, which selectively tolerates, and is openly intolerant of Christians. It postures as a liberator, but it is a tyrant. It preaches freedom, but it means to enslave. It speaks of love, but it loves only those who love it—and woe betide those who do not.

REHABILITATING "TOLERANCE"

How do we rehabilitate this word?

First, we must insist that *tolerance* does not mean *agreement*, nor does *disagreement* mean *intolerance*.

Tolerance, in fact, suggests disagreement, for when you agree with someone, you do not merely tolerate him, you take his side and welcome his opinions. We must patiently explain that disagreement or disapproval of one another's opinions and actions is expected in a secular society where we have been thrown together through the involuntary forces of birth and economics. Peace is preserved by tolerating the opinions, and even actions, of others, although we may, and should be permitted to, voice public disagreement or disapproval.

Second, we must distinguish between private and public intolerance. Private intolerance may consist in disassociating with someone, switching off the radio, closing the browser window, refusing to purchase or sell somewhere, or refusing someone admission to your home. Private intolerance is one of the freedoms individuals have a right to. For a government to deny these individual freedoms is tyranny. And for individuals to call for the abolition of these freedoms is to lend their support to oppression. I cannot expect a secular society to outlaw what I refuse to allow into my own home or private company, if it is not destructive to the society at large, nor can I insist they mandate all that I tolerate or choose. Conversely, unless my speech or activity is physically destructive to persons or property, no government should outlaw what I tolerate in my private capacity. We must maintain a clear distinction between the private freedom to disagree and disassociate, from what governments should be allowed to do by force.

Third, public intolerance (for that is the kind people are really talking about) should usually only be enacted by human government. What a society deems to be intolerable to its existence (murder, theft, treason) can only be removed by the rule of law. Human government is established by God for the preservation of order in human society. However much Christians feel the evil of abortion, no Christian is authorized to enact some form of public intolerance: harming doctors performing abortions, blocking access to abortion clinics, or sabotaging the private property of such places. Vigilante justice only increases the chances of anarchy, which is always followed by tyranny. In times of confusion, Christians of all people should make it clear that public intolerance belongs to the civil authorities.

Finally, Christians should do their utmost to urge that civil law be based upon natural law. As societies abandon transcendent moral principles, they flounder to judge what is genuinely tolerable and intolerable to a society. At such moments, rulers are susceptible to popular opinion, particularly the increasingly vocal opinions of the liberal left. If enough people claim that Christian orthodoxy is hate-speech, rulers may imagine a real threat to society where there is none and make publicly intolerable what ought to be a matter of private intolerance. People don't have to listen to Christian radio stations or read Christian books, but Christians should have the freedom to state Christian ideas in public. As long as those ideas (whether implemented or merely considered) do not incite violence – i.e., public intolerance – the society should tolerate their expression. Natural law will consider whether ideas and their expression harm the public good by considering whether those ideas and expressions are good or evil, and not whether they are popular or acceptable to the prevailing political correctness.

As long as Christians accept the way the word *tolerance* is currently used, we will be slowly strangled by its anti-Christian meanings. Let us graciously challenge error with truth.

CONCLUSION

Satan's first attack on man was to undermine God's Word. "Did God *really* say?" Satan went on to re-define *death* as *life*: "The death God says you will undergo is really an awakening into godlike knowledge. He only calls it 'death' to scare you."

Once *sin* and *death* were redefined as *bravery* and *maturity*, and once Adam and Eve accepted that re-definition, the actual act of sin was much easier.

Indeed, perhaps the first three chapters of Genesis revolve around the meaning of the word "good". God gets to define good as his own estimation of the beauty of his creation. He places Man in the Garden, corrects the only thing "not good" - man's solitariness - and warns them off one prohibited tree. That tree symbolized independent knowledge of what is good, rather than dependent, submissive knowledge of what is good. Once Satan redefined good as "independent, godlike knowledge and power", and Adam and Eve accepted the new definition, the temptation grew in power.

Perhaps all sin begins with unbelief in God's definitions, and belief in distorted ones. For we are creatures made in God's image, and therefore words are central to us. We cannot think without them. We reason through them.

God's Word stands as a bulwark against satanic definitions of *good, life, wisdom, God, sin, evil, love, truth, glory, joy*. Every Sunday, faithful preachers battle against wicked spiritual forces that place false thoughts, ideas, and words into the minds of our people through the world system (2 Cor. 10:5-6).

Right now, the ten words profiled in the book represent battle fronts where plenty of lies are being sown. There are, no doubt, many other words being distorted. But these ten, in my opinion, represent battles worth fighting for the sake of healthy churches, mature Christians and a faithful presence in a darkening world.

Fight for these words. Fight for their true meaning. Fight for truth.